THE SOUTHERN WAY

Issue No 1

CONTENTS

© Kevin Robertson (Noodle Books) and the various contributors 2007

ISBN   (10) 0 –9554110-3-3   (13) 978-0-9554110-3-8

First published in 2007 by Kevin Robertson
under the **NOODLE BOOKS** imprint
PO Box 279
Corhampton
SOUTHAMPTON
SO32 3ZX

www.kevinrobertsonbooks.co.uk

Printed in England by
Ian Allan (Printing) Ltd
Hersham, Surrey

'The Getty Files - 1'

Reminiscent in many ways of the well known New York view of builders on scaffolding high above the City streets, this is Waterloo with workers in the process of demolishing the gantry supporting the former Waterloo 'A' Box after the introduction of colour light signalling in 1936. (See Part 1 of the Waterloo article on pages 38 to 53 of this issue.)

Hulton Archive HM1078-001

Editorial Introduction

Well all I can say is thank-you. Thank you to those of you who purchased the 'Preview' issue and equally those of you who have bought this one and are reading this thus far.

Indeed it seems as if I have struck a cord somewhere and I am grateful to all who have passed comment. Some of this is on the 'Rebuilding' feature on page 65. Let me also say at the outset that I am conscious we will never please all of the people all of the time, but the general consensus seems to be you like the balance, so for the present at least we will try and maintain the same formula.

In commencing the preparation for this issue I had also just about worked out the ratio of articles to photographs to pages, when another box of material arrived. Accordingly I have taken the decision to keep the variety by splitting one of the articles - in this case that on Waterloo. I did not want to have a single piece dominate the whole issue so you will have to wait till next time to see the rest of the photographs on that one.

In going around the shows, it has been a pleasure to talk to many of you and listen to your suggestions for future comment. These we will act on whenever possible but I do not want to change the format - just yet.

What I was keeping my fingers over in particular, was that there would be a supply of new material as a result of the 'Preview Issue'. That has certainly proven to be the case with much arriving from friends old and new - thank you all for your trust. Continuing in the same vein I might add that I had the privilege of visiting one source for material only to be confronted with what were six loco chimneys in the garden being used as plant-pots. Apparently slugs and snails are not yet adept at climbing the side of a 'King Arthur' chimney to get at the hosters. Whilst also not in any way wishing to sound ungrateful, more photographs and articles are still welcome.

Again then this issue should likewise contain pieces most will not have seen, and I can assure you there is plenty more to come! The other thing I have to consider is whether it is worth producing the odd 'Special' from time to time where one topic would otherwise fill a complete issue or it might otherwise be some time before material might be fitted in. There could be some exciting news about this shortly and it will be announced as soon as we can confirm details What I can confirm it will again be all Southern throughout.

I had hoped that there would be room in this issue for an article on the Brighton line re-signalling of the 1930s. Colin Hall, and whose photographs appear on pages 34 and 35 has loaned me some wonderful contemporary information but space constraints mean it will have to held over until a later issue. More on the same topic has come from Irvine Cresswell - Gentlemen thank you, the shortage of signalling material has well and truly been overcome.

I keep also to my original promise that I am more than happy to publicise relevant titles related to the topics covered in 'SW'. This we have done this time, and whilst obviously as a bookseller (- putting one of my other hats on), I am delighted to supply available titles, your local book-shop or trader also needs your support.

With 'SW' setting itself the remit of covering primarily the period 1923-1970, it is frightening to think that the upper end of that timescale is nearly 40 years ago. Indeed this very year we commemorate the sad anniversary of the 40th year since the end of Southern Steam, and yet if we turn the clock back to 1967 and then trace an equivalent 40 years back from there - to 1927, it seems an awfully long way back indeed. I mention that because memories suffers and those survivors from way back become fewer with each passing year.

If you have ever listened to the reminiscing of a former railwayman they can reveal some fascinating stories. I am not suggesting necessarily for print either, but just listen to former staff and they may comment on things the rest of us would never have considered. Next time you are an exhibition do a bit of eavesdropping, you never know what you might find out.

Kevin Robertson

Left: - Ash Level Crossing 1965. The policeman was not remonstrating with the lorry driver over perhaps a missing 'C' licence (- remember them????), but instead just doing an old fashioned bit of gossiping. Clearly it has also attracted the attention of the motorman as he passes by. The photo of course could only be by Rod Hoyle.

Previous page: Demolishing one of the gantries from mechanical signalling day at Waterloo. In context this view has to be very similar to the well known view of construction workers taking a break on a girder high above New York.

Hulton Archive / Getty Images 2674169

Front cover: View of Petworth looking east from the overbridge in 1963. The pick up freight with 33018 is impatient to depart but little of this steam will be needed for the two Grain hoppers, one open wagon and the Brake van which is all there is in today's load.

Terry Cole

Rear cover: LSWR Signals at Basingstoke in the 1960s. These were the down home signals with the station in the background.

Tony Woodford Collection

Two five-car 'Belle' sets led by No 3051 near Haywards Heath on 20th July 1951.
British Railways

THE BRIGHTON BELLE

Antony Ford

Those fortunate enough to have experienced a trip on the electric Brighton Belle in its heyday, particularly first-class, will not fail to remember the old world charm and ambience of the stately Pullman cars. With their stunning individual interiors and attentive service the train conveyed the businessman and day-tripper alike from London Victoria to the coast in under one hour.

Michael Baker once said of his impressions of the Belle that, "… one can excuse the eulogies of the press over the furnishings of the Pullmans for they really were rather sumptuous". Equally, as Nicholas Owen asserts in his 1972 book, "…each car was visibly designed for comfort…the interiors of each of the 15 cars varied in some small detail, it being the Pullman practice to design each car individually…where the woodcuts of pastoral scenes, for example, invariably caught the eye". So how did this wonderful train come about and why, after nearly forty years service, did it retire in 1972?

The origins of Pullman travel on the Brighton line certainly emanated back to the early steam days of the 1870s, and latterly, when the popular and so-called 'most luxurious train in the world' The Southern Belle introduced the first British-built 12 wheel cars of magnificent grace and character on the lines of the former London, Brighton and South Coast Railway.

It was in connection with the electrification of the Southern Railway between London, Brighton and Worthing, which was opened throughout to regular traffic on 1st January 1933, that the Pullman Car Company Limited introduced, what Modern Transport at the time proclaimed, were the "first all-steel electrically-driven multiple-unit Pullman trains embodying new methods of construction, insulation and Ventilation." The trains were part of an order of 38 new cars built at the works of the Metropolitan-Cammell Carriage, Wagon and Finance Company, Limited, Saltley, Birmingham. These attractive vehicles in their distinct umber and cream livery, lined out in gold, were actually longer, wider and loftier than earlier Pullman cars including those all–steel cars introduced in 1928 for the celebrated 'Queen of Scots' (and other prestige services) on the London and North Eastern Railway. Unlike any other Pullman car type in service there were some distinct visual exterior characteristics including the lightly flared contour of the body sides, oval vestibule windows and sliding lights.

The cars were of four standard designs. Three of these types were for the new Southern Belle sets Nos. 2051, 2052 and 2053 and consisting of five Pullman cars (latterly to become the Brighton Belle): two of which were motor brakes, seating 48 third-class passengers (tare weight of 62 tons and length over buffers 68 ft. 8.75 ins); a parlour car seating 56 third-class (tare weight of 39 tons and length over vestibules 66 ft) and two first-class kitchen cars each seating 20 (tare weight 43 tons and length over vestibules 66 ft). Interestingly, the third-class seating with its cramped two and two arrangement contrasted unfavourably with the relatively new steam hauled cars used in the Bournemouth Belle, Queen of Scots and other services, with their two and one abreast configuration, but on reflection, the short journey time arguably allowed for reasonable comfort in what were seen as luxurious appointments. In service, the operating pattern was generally two units in use and with one spare.

The remaining 23 vehicles were composite Pullman kitchen cars that were formed in the express units on the London – South Coast services offering an ingenious arrangement of first and third-class accommodation; each unique with interior schemes of striking pictorial and geometric effects that clearly reflected some of the best craftsmanship of the time and each car was also bestowed a name: Ethel, Daisy, Olive, Peggy, and so on.

In all instances, the question of insulation, both against noise and change of temperature, had drawn special consideration. The floors, for example, were

insulated with cork and on the body sides and roof 'insulwood' was employed, resulting in an effective arrangement whereby trial reports evidently indicated that even at the highest speeds conversation was maintained without undue effort. The buffers, gangways, drawgear and bogies were to the designs and requirements of the Southern Railway but clearly marked "Pullman".

As with all Pullman cars running in services throughout England, Scotland and Southern Ireland during the 1930s, they were generally regarded by the travelling public as being synonymous for their luxurious appointments, particularly first-class, but a supplement was nearly always levied for their use. The interior arrangements of the 'Belle' cars were, however, regarded as very different from that of Pullman cars previously constructed and quickly gained a following.

From a mechanical perspective, the power for lighting at 70 volts was supplied from motor generators mounted on the motor cars, providing lighting for the whole of the train and also power control. The lighting scheme on all cars was particularly attractive. In the first-class saloons for instance, the arrangement was quite unique and consisted of strip lighting on either side throughout the length of each saloon sporting peach coloured frosted glass etched with a stylish zig zag sun-ray effect that was so redolent of the Art-Deco influence

of the 1930s as often replicated, too, in other railway company vehicles, notably, the LNER's 'Flying Scotsman'.

Digressing slightly, this same style was subsequently taken further in other forms of transport including the shipping companies' flag ships, like the Queen Mary or the Normandie.

The general impression from contemporary reports and railway related journals was extremely good, and as expected, much attention was made to promote the aesthetic achievements which were invariably in evidence when new cars with their innovative interiors were being introduced into service. For example, the 1924 inauguration of the short-lived 'Sheffield Pullman' had much publicity surrounding the striking Japanese lacquer panels of first-class car 'Geraldine'. Interestingly, for those who were comfort conscious, the ends of the first-class passenger saloons had been so designed as to form small alcoves, thus providing additional privacy for passengers occupying seats in the vicinity of the doorways.

Modern Transport states that the opportunity was taken to introduce a "delightful concealed lighting effect on the end saloon marquetry panel work". Within each first-class car, as was virtually always the case – particularly in vehicles from at least 1910 - an enclosed coupe compartment seating four had similar strip

Left: Front end view of a new motor coach and as originally numbered. It was this unit which was badly damaged in an air-raid at Victoria on 9th/10th October 1940 and was subsequently returned to the builders for repair.
The 1940s had also seen some of the Pullman cars repainted in an all-over brown livery. From 4th May 1942 all the sets were taken out of use and it is believed, stored initially at Epsom Goods. Sets 3051 and 3053 returned to service on 1st May 1946 in their original livery but even so it was commonplace to see a '5-Bel' set coupled to a '6-Pul' until set 3052 was again available for traffic and the full service resumed on 6th October 1947.

Right: Construction detail of the new all-steel Pullman vehicles.

Both: 'Railway Gazette'.

(The 'Railway Gazette' published a supplement on 30th December 1932 entirely devoted to electrification on the Southern Railway between London, Brighton, and Worthing.)

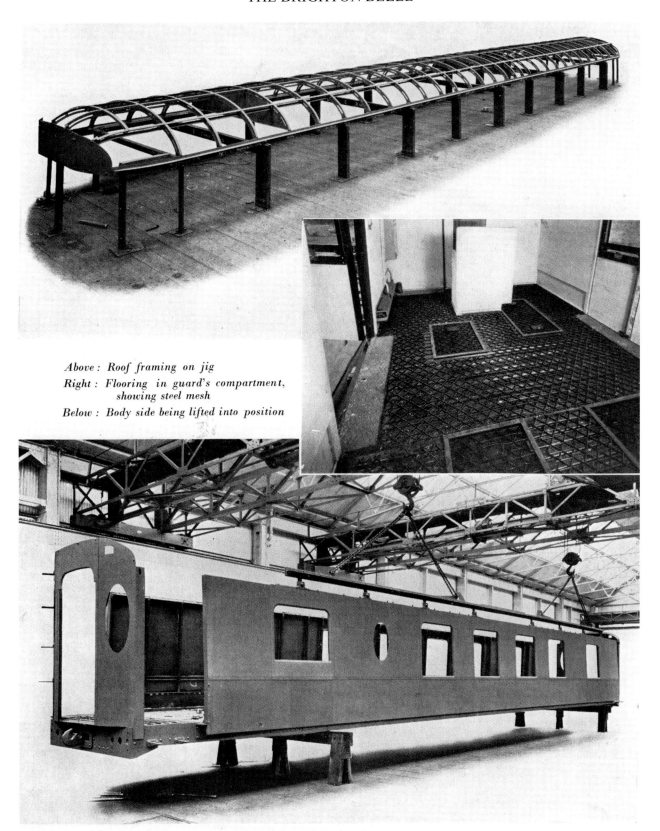

Above : Roof framing on jig
Right : Flooring in guard's compartment, showing steel mesh
Below : Body side being lifted into position

ASSEMBLY OF ALL-STEEL PULLMAN CAR

lighting to that in the main saloons, but the glass panels were built into the cornice. Following the practice established in 1915 with the introduction of third-class cars, only those vehicles conveying first-class (or an element of first-class) accommodation were named, the third-class cars bearing their Pullman numbers on the side panels, flanked both sides by the Pullman company crest. Thus, the names bestowed upon the Belle first-class cars - Hazel, Doris, Audrey, Vera, Mona and Gwen - were names from the fashion of the 1930s and nowadays, of course, date them as precisely as their interiors.

By comparison, the third-class accommodation featured semi-recessed ceiling lights with opaque glass tulip shades and panel-type bracket lights between seats with decorated glass forming a similar sun ray effect to that in first-class. In both classes all tables were equipped with rather stunning table lamps – a veritable hallmark of Pullman travel -originally rendered in a satin silver finish to harmonise with all the metalwork. Certainly, the Belle first-class versions accentuated Art-Deco overtures with an elegant form and heavily flared octagonal base, the third-class type were, however, plain with a circular base, but nevertheless were as equally elegant topped off with a so-called 'unbreakable' shade made of celluloid - a relatively new material in 1933 - in varying colours over the years in the form of a tulip. For the service of refreshments and meals, a "specially attractive and compact electric cooking range" was positioned in each first-class car. As reported by Modern Transport "visible from the corridor [the range was] faced with polished stainless steel beading, with handles and other fittings in chromium plate".

The ventilation of all cars had been the subject of great deliberation, and unlike many of the older Pullmans by then running in their twentieth year, the electric Pullmans promoted many special features, hitherto unknown, including an automatic rejection of incoming smoke from steam locomotives, and a thermostatic control to regulate the temperature in each car. Passengers were able to observe by means of a glass encased illuminated thermometer – outside the lavatory in each corridor - the temperature of the outside atmosphere and that within the car.

The lavatories, too, were well designed and employed large 'eau-de-nil polychrome' panels with black beading and featuring one large oval mirror. The wash basins were in black porcelain and all fittings chromium plated. For a time there were clothes brushes and also scented liquid soap. The vestibules and corridors were finished in Cuban mahogany and the floors in the lavatories, corridors, vestibules and third-class saloons were covered with interlocking rubber tiling in grey and green, and linoleum of the best quality for the passenger accommodation. First-class saloons were finished out in rich deep pile carpets of varied colours to harmonise with the surrounding decoration. Four firms had been responsible for the interior decoration of the cars, including Waring & Gillow and Maple & Co.

In recent years, several excellent publications on "Pullman" history have recorded that after eighteen months following the start of electric services, the train was officially re-named the 'Brighton Belle' and to avoid confusion with the newly-introduced 'Bournemouth Belle'. As Nicholas Owen remarks:- "It was a sign of the way Brighton had taken the train to its heart that the formal re-christening ceremony was carried out on 29th June 1934, by Miss M Hardy, Brighton's Mayor".

By the end of the 1930s, contemporary photographs show the interiors with vibrantly coloured and jazz-patterned moquette on the seats and large white crisp antimacassars. Progressively through the Belle's life, the interiors displayed slight changes in what appears to be the Pullman Car Company's attempt at keeping up with fashion trends, deploying occasionally plain or sombre seat moquette, whilst post-war, decorative fixed curtains were introduced and the clocks were removed - having been replaced by an attractive wooden plaque sporting the Pullman coat of arms and the name or number of the car.

Following the outbreak of war in September 1939, many Pullman and restaurant cars were prematurely withdrawn. Some were reinstated on a limited service including the Belle; by 1942 there was, however, no justification for running luxury services and most Pullmans were sent off to storage for the duration.

Opposite Page : Top left - Drivers compartment. This was identical with the contemporary 'Corridor' and 'City' sets introduced around the same time.

Opposite Page - Top right - Vestibule end by Messrs Spencer Moulton and who were also responsible other rubber components as well as the buffers. Both 'Railway Gazette'

Opposite Page - Lower: Brighton circa 1938, set 3053 awaiting departure with the 5.25 pm to Victoria. The schedule was nearly always set at one hour in either direction and for what was a non-stop run.

3ʀᴅ Cʟ. Mᴏᴛᴏʀ Bʀᴀᴋᴇ. Wᴇɪɢʜᴛ 62 Tᴏɴs. 48 Sᴇᴀᴛs.	3ʀᴅ Cʟ. Pᴀʀʟᴏᴜʀ Cᴀʀ. Wᴇɪɢʜᴛ 39 Tᴏɴs. 56 Sᴇᴀᴛs.	1ꜱᴛ Cʟ. Kɪᴛᴄʜᴇɴ Cᴀʀ. Wᴇɪɢʜᴛ 43 Tᴏɴs. 20 Sᴇᴀᴛs.	1ꜱᴛ Cʟ. Kɪᴛᴄʜᴇɴ Cᴀʀ. Wᴇɪɢʜᴛ 43 Tᴏɴs. 20 Sᴇᴀᴛs.	3ʀᴅ Cʟ. Mᴏᴛᴏʀ Bʀᴀᴋᴇ. Wᴇɪɢʜᴛ 62 Tᴏɴs. 48 Sᴇᴀᴛs.

SOUTHERN BELLE. 3 UNITS.

Opposite page- top: First class car 'Mona' and which was paired with 'Gwen' in set No 3053. (Other First-class pairings were, 'Hazel' and 'Doris' in 3051, and 'Audrey' and 'Vera' in 3052.)

Opposite page lower: Third class parlour No 85 also from 3053. (No 86 was in 3051, and No 87 in 3053.)

Above: First class accommodation - showing the interior of 'Gwen'. The clocks in the vehicles were from 'Smith's English Clock Ltd' and were identical in 3rd class. All were removed post-war.
Left - centre and lower: Variations in furnishings within the third class vehicles. Motor Car 90 (above) and trailer Car 85 (below).
Below: The platform archway at Platform 17 of Victoria Station.

Above: Part of a 1960s BR advert for the two Southern Region Pullman trains. The original showed the Pullman vehicles in their true colours but with the text 'The Brighton Belle' against an attractive red background.

Sadly one unit, No 3052, (formerly 2052), including Audrey and Vera was badly damaged during an air raid on Victoria station, which also apparently destroyed many of the records at the offices of the Pullman Car Company. The majority of Pullmans were sent to storage often in desolate locations during the interregnum. With the cessation of hostilities, the Pullman Company made a sterling effort to reintroduce many former services and inaugurate new ones, most notably the Devon Belle. During the early post-war years the Brighton Belle – as well as many other Pullman services - became rather popular and featured in the daily routine of many South Coast commuters who took breakfast coming up to London, and a somewhat rushed dinner going down to the coast.

At week-ends, day trippers – who sought something a little more special often - opted for the Pullman, happy to pay the two or three Shillings supplement (from 1971 supplements 20p and 30p respectively) for the personal attention provided by the attendants and, of course, additional comfort. Remarkably, on occasions during the holiday periods the Belle became fully booked and would-be Pullman passengers were turned away or opted for the Pullman composites. In 1963, British Railways Southern Region offered a 'Rail-Belle' ticket which included supper on

Set 3051 approaching Haywards Heath on 8th May 1955.

Final BR corporate livery for set No 3053 seen at Waterloo on 8th April 1972 in connection an RCTS Railtour. Special workings with the sets were a semi-regular feature throughout their lives and as such the sets visited a number of locations across the electrified network as far west as Portsmouth.   *John Scrace*

the 11pm train (stopping at Haywards Heath) at an all-in charge of 36 shillings 1st Class, 27 shillings 2nd Class. (This increased the Belle's diagrammed workings weekdays to four return trips). There was even a specially constructed arch proclaiming 'Brighton Belle' on Platform 17 at Victoria station.

More than anything else, the Belle became famous for its clientele, as Nicholas Owen remarks. Passengers included celebrities like Flora Robson, Lawrence Olivier, Dora Bryan and satirist Alan Melville. Certainly by the mid 1960s the train had a reportedly distinct dancing gait when travelling at speed which was most noticeable over points and evident particularly in the motor cars, and despite the fact that £70,000 had been spent on replacing the bogies in the mid 1950s, this declining condition and the aged non-standard equipment by the early 1970s contributed in part to the decision to axe the train altogether.

However, the Belle did receive a major overhaul beginning late 1968 and into 1969 and the opportunity was taken - rightly or wrongly - to make the train conform to the corporate identity of ordinary British Railways passenger trains. The brand-name of "Pullman" was seemingly becoming faded and could not compete with the modernity of InterCity travel with its sleek new rolling stock promoting not only airconditioning on certain lines, but fast supplement-free services. During the 1960s, the Brighton line was in the process of being upgraded, and sadly much of the pre-war stock disappeared, including by June 1966 the Pullman composite cars.

Equally, to some passengers the Pullman image was from another age; certainly many resented paying the supplementary charge, and inevitably serious consideration was taken to review the Belle's future in light of spiralling staffing and catering costs.

Resplendent in blue and grey livery, and with bright orange curtains, new seating material and redesigned lamp shades, the Brighton Belle soldiered on until April 1972 when it was withdrawn after much celebration including a 'Champagne supper' and the cars sold for preservation.

As Alan Melville remarked in 1972 (quoted by Nicholas Owen):-"...The Belle was much more than a train; it was almost a club. [You] were greeted by a cheerful steward, shown into one of those armchairs, looked at almost in awe for the thousandth time at those incredible examples of inlaid woodwork in the panelling, and regarded with affection the lampshade on the spotless linen on your table. You felt, even before the train pulled out of the Victoria, that you were at home...".

QUESTIONS - QUESTIONS?

CAN YOU HELP...?

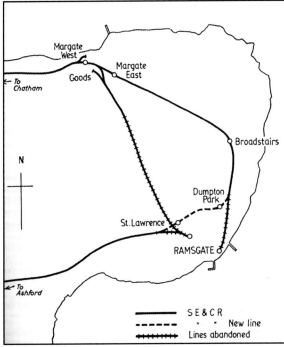

(Both the Town and Harbour stations at Ramsgate were closed from 2nd July 1926 and replaced by a single new station on a new site from the same date.)

Every so often photographs turn up which throw up questions. Where, when, and for what reason etc. etc. Three are shown here, someone must know the answers so over to you please. (It is not a competition as such although I am confident someone can help....)

Starting on this page, we know it is WW2 and the ladies are part of the Eastleigh outside paint gang who had replaced the men for 'the duration'. Most were not local and were billeted in 'digs' around the Eastleigh area. All we know is that they never went away overnight and so it must be within daily travelling distance - but where is it, SR or even GW!!!? With just a piece of track and what may be taken to be the platform fencing there is not much to go on. Any suggestions please? *Photo Jim Langrish collection*

Opposite page top: - We know where it is, Ramsgate Town, and although the view has been seen once before this scan is from an original postcard and not a copy. Obviously it is also sometime after 1898 due to the SECR notice. But does anyone know the circumstances?

Photo Dave Hammersley collection

Opposite page lower: - This time it is a not dissimilar indent at the Harbour Station but involving 'D' class 4-4-0 No 92. Again any suggestions please? (Bradley refers to an incident involving No 92 at Dover - was he getting mixed up?)

Photo Lens of Sutton collection

FLASHBACK

IS THIS THE ANSWER TO THE WINCHESTER PROBLEM?

Roger Simmonds

This photograph of Adams "135" Class 4-4-0 No. 146 at the head of a train composed of Great western stock has been described over the years as being located on the Didcot, Newbury & Southampton line near Winchester. However it's exact location has never properly been defined and certain features contained in the view call into question this supposition.

What is certain is that the pictures was taken between 1892 and about 1897, gleaned from the short lived engine head code bracket fitted on the smoke box door seen above the handles which were generally removed from the engine stock from 1896. Using this datum point we move to the location problem.

If this train is on the DN&S the use of an LSWR engine and GWR carriage stock suggests it is between Winchester and Shawford Junction as few (if any) through workings by South Western locomotives north of Winchester took place at this time. Supporting this is the train head code configuration which is correct,

and probably led to the original description. However this cannot be the case as firstly there are no over bridges on this section, and secondly the signalling layouts at Shawford Junction and Winchester do not conform with the signal visible beyond the bridge and the signal wire seen in the foreground.

Could the location be north of Winchester GWR?. Supporting this theory would again be the engine head code and the ¾ mile post to the right of the engine, which if the 24 ¾ mile post, would place the train conveniently approaching the tunnel north of the station in the Winnall area. However there are difficulties here as the over bridge is not of the right type with that provided at Easton Lane nor the location of the worked signal. Closer examination reveals that the bridge detail is unfamiliar with any on the DN&S and the permanent way does not appear to be of the GWR type which soon replaced much of the original DN&S inside keyed track on the running line.

18

So was this picture taken on the DN&S?. So far the evidence would suggest not, but how about the head code carried. The position of the discs are clearly correct for the Winchester – Shawford Junction route, but further examination suggests that the crosses on the discs are significant. The use of red and black crosses from about 1892 to 1900 was to enable a greater variety of route descriptions to be used as the LSWR system expanded. Thus the same disc positions with plain or cross variations denoted different diagrammed routes. Reference to the official 1892 head code descriptions does not show a configuration matching the one in the photograph, but as from time to time supplementary allocations were given, the list was probably not exhaustive.

By 1901 the use of crosses on discs had been dispensed with being replaced by the use of diamond shaped discs. A considerable number of these were direct replacements for the former use of crossed discs. Perhaps the search for the true location of our view could be aided if an initial assumption is made that this was the case here. Taking the 1901 replacement list, this head code would indicate a service between Portsmouth and Salisbury via Netley and Southampton West.

At this time the line from Fareham to St Denys was single track so this is feasible (the second running line was opened on 10th April 1910). A careful study of the 25" Ordnance Survey for the period limits the location to one possibility, that being east of Bitterne station looking at a Southampton to Portsmouth train (probably originating from Cardiff or Bristol). There are many favourable indications which strongly support this view:

- The train formation composed of GWR stock was commonplace on these through services, usually of 5 to 6 carriages (the DN&S route was rarely more than 3).
- The over bridge matches exactly with Occupation Bridge No. 4 south of the Itchen Road Bridge. This is also verified on official SR plans.
- The signal beyond the bridge would be Bitterne's Down Advanced Starter and the wire leading in the foreground controls the Up Distant Signal.
- The land contours leading into a cutting, shallow on the Up side and deeper on the Down side are correct.
- The ¾ mile post is accurately positioned in relation to the over bridge and represents 2 ¾ miles from Southampton Town.

The head code issue is open to question however, and an assumption has been made in this case on the transition from crossed to diamond shaped discs. I hope I have solved the mystery of this picture, but if anyone has any further information which adds to the debate it would be most welcome.

I would like to acknowledge the help of Reg Randall for his assistance and advice in this research.

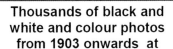

THE GETTY FILES

Grove Road, Deptford, on the south bank of the Thames and on a unreported date, although certainly pre WW2.

The actual location is near the junction with Hanlon Street visible in the left background and whilst Hanlon Street has not existed for some years, Grove Road still survives and is now designated the B206.

The 'D1' tank is heading towards the former City of London Corporation Cattle Market, latterly Government Stores Yard (No 3 base supply depot), and with the service originating off the LBSCR Deptford Wharf Branch.

The factory on the left belongs to A G Scott & Co, whilst the Dennis lorry is lettered 'Harrison Rogers Ltd. Swedish Wharf, Fulham. Box and Packing case Makers'.

Special instructions running to a whole page in the 1934 SR Sectional Appendix were printed relative to these workings and which also refer to the location as being Grove Street.

These notices include reference to two engines being used, a four-coupled at the stores end and a six-coupled engine at the rear - hence the cloud of steam also visible. The six-coupled engine was not permitted to work inside the Stores Yard.

Trains would run ' as required' and were limited to 25 wagons including brake van preceded at no more than 5 mph by a man with a red flag.

Night time working would see the front engine having to have two headlamps one at each end of the buffer beam.

Hulton Archive / Fox Photos / Getty Images JB7971-001

(Comment on the workings of this branch in its latter days is made on page 49 of the 'R.O.' for February 1956.)

2695 at Exmouth Junction 27th May 1948. A study of this and other views reveals variations in the shape and size of the balance weights fitted to the driving axles. It is tempting then to suppose such changes only affected the engines that were rebalanced and as described in the text although this does not correspond with the available photographs or information.   *R K Blencowe Collection*

No. 2608 - the former 'Jersey' at an unreported location. The small piece of loose pipe hanging down from the top of the firebox appears in more than one view and was a drain from within the cab..   *KR Collection*

More information specifically on the 'Torrington & Marland Light Railway' and referred to by Rod Garner in this article can be found in Rod's 2006 book on the 'T & M' published by Kestrel Railway Books.

Ramblings on, and of:

THE E1/R 0-6-2 TANK ENGINES

Rod Garner

The first of William Stroudley's E1 class of local goods and shunting 0-6-0Ts left the London Brighton & South Coast Railway Company's works at Brighton in 1874. The class came to number some 61 engines, with a surprisingly large number of these carrying names. With 4' 6" wheels they apparently provided good service over the years, although when used for passenger duties and running at any sort of speed it appears they were not popular with either crews or passengers. Withdrawals also commenced as early as 1908 although this was destined to be a long drawn out procedure and would continue sporadically over the next 50 years

On its incorporation in 1923, the Southern Railway had inherited a motley collection of locomotives from its constituent companies, and soon began investigating the need to rationalise and update its motive power resources. This was especially so in the difficult terrain of the West Country noted for its tight curves and steep gradients. A classic illustration of the problem was the operation of the North Devon and Cornwall Junction Light Railway from Torrington to Halwill Junction, which opened in 1925 and was worked by the Southern. The early part of the line to Torrington was reasonably well engineered as far as gradients and curves were concerned, but the line south towards Halwill Junction ran over the track bed of the former Torrington & Marland narrow gauge line and was far less conducive to easy running. More powerful motive power for this and other West Country branches able to take the new 16 ton maximum axle load was urgently needed although this was only available with the pair of

No 2696 at Barnstaple Junction on 18th August 1935. The use of the type as banking engines at Exeter was so successful that they would completely replace the smaller 'G6' engines on this work.

R S Carpenter / H F Wheeler Collection

LBSC Number & Name		Built	SR number	BR number	Rebuilt to E1/R	Rebuilding rder No and Date		Date Withdrawn
94	Shorewell	Nov 1883	B94 / 2094	32094	May 1927	B230	13/1/27	April 1955
95	Luccombe	Nov 1883	B95 / 2095	32095	May 1927	B230	13/1/27	Nov. 1956
96	Salzberg	Dec 1883	B96 / 2096	32096	Oct. 1928	B328	10/5/28	Nov. 1956
99 / 610	Bordeaux *	Dec 1874	B610 / 2610	32610	Jan. 1929	B328	10/5/28	March 1953
103 / 695	Normandy	Sept 1876	B695 / 2695	32695	Oct. 1928	B328	10/5/28	Feb. 1957
104 / 696	Brittany	Oct 1876	B696 / 2696	32696	Dec. 1928	B328	10/5/28	Jan. 1956
105 / 697	Morlaix	Sept 1876	B696 / 2697	32697	Jan. 1929	B328	10/5/28	Nov. 1959
108 / 608	Jersey	Nov 1876	B608 / 2608	32608	Nov. 1928	B328	10/5/28	May 1957
124	Bayonne	Aug 1878	B124 / 2124	32124	Dec. 1928	B328	10/5/28	Jan. 1959
135	Foligno	Jan 1879	B135 / 2135	32135	Nov. 1928	B328	10/5/28	March 1959

* as No 99 carried the name 'Loco Dept. Brighton from about 1909 to 1922.

former Plymouth, Devonport & South Western Junction Railway 0-6-2T locos, one of which No. 758 "Lord St. Levan" was sent to Torrington for trials and reportedly performed well. Accordingly the makers, Hawthorn Leslie & Co. Ltd. were asked to tender for six new engines.

The cost of these was clearly too much for the Southern's accountants and instead the idea was mooted to convert ten surplus E1 engines into 0-6-2 radial tanks. The cost saving in so doing was quoted at £12,500. The main difficulty to be faced was to increase the water supply over a new pony truck whilst at the same time keeping the overall weight within the limits specified by the Chief Civil Engineer. Design work was undertaken at Brighton and successfully resulted in the use of an 'N' class pony truck above which the main frames were extended rearwards to accommodate a larger bunker of 2¼ ton capacity and also an additional 348 gallons bringing the new water capacity to 1,260 gallons which included a well tank. The Westinghouse brake was also changed to vacuum, the reservoirs for which were carried either side of the bunker below the framing. Other changes included the provision of injectors compared with feed pumps. A new cab with definite SECR contours was also fitted.

Brighton Works was also responsible for the actual rebuilding, Nos 94 and 95 the first to be altered in May 1927, and which were tested on local routes. According to Bradley. "...once the odd [unspecified] teething trouble had been overcome..", the first two engines were despatched to the West Country. The remaining eight engines being dealt with at Brighton between October 1928 and January 1929.

Allocations varied but initially Nos 2094 and 2696 went to Exmouth Junction for shunting and pilot duties - although quickly after this the pair were sent to the sub-shed at Torrington. The remaining eight (numbers 2095 / 2096 / 2124 / 2135 / 2608 / 2610 / 2695 / 2697) went straight to Barnstaple. They performed well on the hilly terrain of the Halwill to Torrington section. Unfortunately on the better alignment of the Torrington to Barnstaple section higher speeds were attained and which caused them to oscillate with a 'fore and aft' motion. Since they were originally built for slow goods and shunting work this is hardly surprising! Accordingly the complaints of rough riding first voiced years ago surfaced again, not now from the crews but instead just from passengers. Accordingly five of the class, Nos 2096, 2094, 2095, 2608, and 2610 were rebalanced between May 1936 and August 1937. After this these five engines were based at Barnstaple for use on Halwill and Torrington line passenger services. Those not modified were kept for shunting at the fairly extensive sidings at Fremington Quay, station pilot duty, and also work from Exmouth Junction, which from 1938 including banking between the GW and SR stations at Exeter.

But even with their increased water capacity the E1/Rs could not work all the way to Halwill without refilling at Hatherleigh, and on the occasions when the water supply at Hatherleigh failed another locomotive had to be found for the service – an Adams 0-6-0 if available. The E1/Rs managed quite adequately with the traffic on the line to Halwill Junction which was rarely more than mundane, but they were however restricted to fifteen loaded wagons plus a brake van between Torrington and Peters Marland and nineteen plus brake from Peters Marland to Halwill Junction. In adverse weather conditions, or when overloaded, the skills of the engine crew could be severely tested on this rather remote little route. Like the railway itself, the E1/Rs soon became an established part of the local scene, which they shared with a few M7 4-4-0 tank locomotives and even the occasional Bulleid light pacific which had presumably taken the left fork at Barnstaple Junction rather than the right turn to Ilfracombe!

During mid 1941, two engines, Nos 2608 and 2610 spent some time at Plymouth although all survived to have 30000 added to their numbers by BR. 32094 was

Above: - No 2610 at Torrington on an unreported date. The reservoir at the rear underneath the bunker was for vacuum and was repeated on the opposite side.   *Both - R K Blencowe*

Below: - No 32095 in lined black BR livery at Barnstaple Junction in 1952. Although theoretically possible to have been carried, no views have emerged showing the class with the later BR crest on the tank sides. Possibly the photograph was taken during the summer months as the steam-heat hose has been removed from the buffer beam.

*Opposite page: -
With the remains
of the timber
viaduct from the
erstwhile
'Torrington &
Marland Light
Railway'
alongside, No
2124 crosses the
modern
replacement with a
Torrington service.
In the background
the topography is
of the Clement
Hill.*

*The Lens of Sutton
Collection*

*This page, above: - No 2094 approaching Barnstaple Junction with a service from Torrington on 18th August 1935.
Included in the formation and nearest the engine is set No 506, of LBSCR origin. The third vehicle could likewise be
from the LBSR. It is possible those at the rear were through coaches - judging from the roof-boards. Notice also the
loco number on the rear of the bunker.*   *R S Carpenter / H F Wheeler Collection*

*This page - lower: In sparkling clean livery, No. 2610 at Torrington, circa 1934. This is possibly a Bideford service
and which would have temporarily backed clear to allow shunting to take place before re-entering the station.*
            The Lens of Sutton Collection

Left: - As BR No 32124 possibly recorded at Eastleigh. This engine has the larger balance weights fitted and yet according to the records was not altered!

KR Collection

This page, centre: - Banking duties for No 32135 at Exeter St David's on 8th July 1958. Plans had once existed for the SR to have its own 'High Level' station at St David's and which route would then have continue crossing the GWR main line at Cowley Bridge before regaining its original alignment towards Crediton.

R K Blencowe Collection

This page, lower: - On the type of duty for which the class were intended, 32696 at Halwill Junction in 1952. The engines were not fitted for push-pull work.

R K Blencowe Collection

Opposite page: - 32124 at Exeter St David's on 1st June 1956 and complete with a spare coupling. The larger balance weights show up well in this view. The new trailing wheels for the class were 3' 1" diameter and were originally spare parts produced at Woolwich Arsenal when the 'N' class had been built.

R K Blencowe Collection

transferred permanently to Plymouth in October 1949 with the remaining E1/Rs continuing as before until replaced by modern Ivatt Class 2 tanks in the spring of 1953. Apart from 32095, 32096, and 32696. the remaining engines were transferred to Exmouth Junction for use on banking duties. 32095 and 32096 were similarly transferred to Plymouth by the autumn of 1955. 32696 was retained at Barnstaple for shunting as before.

Overhauls were still being undertaken in

	Final Mileage	Dark Green	Light Green	Black	Date to BR Lined Black - if known	Re-balanced	Smokebox plate fitted
32094			21/12/40	28/2/46		Yes	27/11/48
32095	1,497,037		4/1/41	9/12/44		Yes	3/7/48
32096				23/5/42 24/12/46	never	Yes	11/9/48
32610			26/10/40	7/9/46	never	Yes	22/1/49
32695		9/40	28/9/40	8/11/47			27/1/51
32696			13/4/40	24/5/41 11/5/46	9/50		29/1/49
32697	1,541,086			22/2/47			14/7/51
32608		13/4/40		17/6/43 20/9/47		Yes	
32124	1,482,336	2/12/39					
32135	1,120,221			5/4/41			's' prefix from March to May 1948 1948.

1954/5, usually at Eastleigh but around that time pressure of work in Hampshire resulted in three engines making works visits to Brighton instead. Shortage of motive power was obviously not an issue affecting steam in the final years either, as following a works visit to Brighton in August 1954, 32695 was 'borrowed' for use on a permanent way train to Tunbridge Wells. Similarly 32697, and the last of the class to survive in service, was despatched under steam from Exmouth

Junction bound for Ashford in the autumn of 1959 but was also commandeered to double head a permanent way train from Salisbury to Eastleigh en-route. Somehow it also managed to spend a month up to the 22nd November 1959 employed on carriage and pilot duties at Eastbourne until eventually reaching Ashford on 4th December 1959.

The author and publisher acknowledge the help of Eric Youldon in the preparation of this article,

Opposite page - top: 17th May 1950, and a view of classic mixed train behind No 32095 climbing the 1 in 67 gradient up from Torrington Viaduct. This view may be compared with that on page 26, where the course of the route around a wide sweeping curve can be noted.

M Whitehouse Collection

Opposite page - lower: On the same date No 32696 has charge of the 10.30 am freight from Barnstaple Junction to the sidings at Marland and is seen climbing the 1 in 67 incline. The variations in livery, although with both engines having BR identification will be noted. This engine received lined black livery four months later. This particular engine was destined to become the last of the class to remain at Barnstaple. A similar view of this same serice but on a different day appeared in the Ian Allan Publication. 'Branch Line Album'.

M Whitehouse Collection

This page: - Further freight working No 32608 at Petrockstow on 24th May 1952.

T J Edgington / Roger Carpenter Collection

Above: -The delightfully sylvan setting of Watergate Halt, No 32696 is leaving with the single coach 3.55pm Torrington to Halwill train on 16th May 1950. In later years the passenger service worked by the E1Rs on this route was restricted to either two or three passengers trains each way, the 20 odd mile journey occupying no less than one and half hours inclusive of seven intermediate stops.   *M Whitehouse Collection*

Above: - Hardly exacting work for No 32610 paused for a water stop at Hatherleigh This was the only other 'main' station on the route between Halwill and Torrington and the existence of the open air lever frame immediately adjacent to the man on the ground will be noted.

T J Edgington / Roger Carpenter Collection

Below: - A fine study of 32697 at Exeter Central on 17th August 1957, by which time the three surviving members of the class were based at nearby Exmouth Junction. Views of the left sides of the class are for whatever reason, not as common as the opposite side and it should be noted this engine has at some stage acquired a plate to the top of the bunker on this side at least, as well as a pronounced droop at the front end! *R K Blencowe Collection*

Opposite page - lower: The classic view of a pair of the class at the rear of a ballast train from Meldon on the steep incline towards Exeter Central. Unfortunately only the leading engine can be identified and which is No 32124. 31st August 1949.

M Whitehouse Collection

William Edward Hall was born in the Norfolk village of Sparham, between Norwich and Fakenham, in 1882. Following schooling he was known to be working as a Water Bailiff but evidently this was not to his liking as by 1901 he was living with his sister in London and working as a Laundryman. Again this was to be short lived for by 1907 he was married and a Fireman for the LBSCR at New Cross, living in Hatcham Park Road not far from the shed. He would later move his home to Forest Hill.

Possibly in an effort to gain early promotion he is known to have been a Motorman, at first working on the 'Brighton Overhead' circa 1912 and certainly by the late 1920's at least was working trains to and from Brighton. Whether he remained solely on electric stock or was in a 'dual-link' is not clear.

Two photographs of his time as a steam man have survived and are reproduced here with the grateful permission of Colin Hall. In both of the views William is shown as the man on the footplate - the identity of the other member of staff on 'Haslemere' is not recorded.

'Carshalton' was a 'D' class tank engine built at Brighton as one of a batch of nine similar engines between March and

November 1875. Originally carrying the number 20, it was renumbered 79, in February 1907 and renumbered further, 79A, in November 1909. Latterly as SR No 3216 the engine lasted in service until August 1933. Notice in particular the wagon alongside, the scan is to the extreme left hand edge of the print but even so it clearly shows up the chalked wording, "...special for test" - and presumably referring to loco coal? The wooden brake-blocks of the engine will be noted.

'Haslemere' No 398, was one of the last pair of D3 tank engines built at Brighton in November 1896. In October 1905 a replacement boiler of the type seen was fitted and which differed from the original by having direct loading safety valves above the firebox. At the same time the engine was repainted on the instructions of the then Locomotive Superintendent, Mr Marsh, in Stroudley's 'Goods Green'. This type of boiler was only carried until October 1908 and meaning it is possible to date the view as being sometime within a three year period, possibly even more exactly 1907/8. The engine was photographed outside the Middle Shed at New Cross. It would survive in traffic for some years and was withdrawn by BR in March 1949.

Notice also on both engines the home shed is written on the framing just behind the buffer beam. *'Carshalton'* displaying 'NEW +' and on *'Haslemere'* 'BTN'.

William Hall retired from the Southern Railway in 1947 still working as a Motorman on the Central Section suburban routes.

Notes and photographs from the archive of Colin Hall.

More from the lens of the master - Rod Hoyle. Rod's work in the Preview Issue of 'SW' has aroused much comment and we are certain these two pages will do likewise. (See page 4 as well.) Further views will appear in later issues. Don't forget an album of Rod Hoyle unique photographs, 'THE ATMOSPHERIC SOUTHERN' is now available. (Details on the inside front cover.)

- and I almost forgot, I am sure most will recognise the locations, but just in case, left is the up side platform at Winchester City, above the 'up' 'Bournemouth Belle' passing St Cross, south of Winchester, and below, Alresford in BR days.

WATERLOO

LSWR to BR

a brief summary

Kevin Robertson

(Part 1. Part 2 will feature in the January Issue)

Waterloo on 27th September 1919, and the first day of the railway strike which lasted for nine days until 5th October.

The view was recorded by the Topical Press photographer as the 12.30 pm to Portsmouth via Woking and Guildford was about to leave Platform 5.

According to Faulkner & Williams just one or two trains daily operated on the main lines.

'A12' No 539 had been built in April 1888 and lasted in service until September 1930. The same number was later allocated to a Maunsell 'Q' class loco,

Above: - The exterior of the former Central Station at Waterloo recorded at noon, 1st February 1911. Directly ahead is the cab-road serving the Main Line arrivals platform and also the North station. Above, the wooden building housed season ticket staff. That to the left is the connection with the SECR and which was as described by O S Nock as "...like a horizontal jet of water from the mouth of a gargoyle" - see main text. Another un-named writer is quoted by Jackson as referring to Waterloo as, "...a jumble of shabby, poverty-stricken buildings...quite unique in London, although quite in keeping with the squalid neighbourhood surrounding it.'

Left: - The South Western Circle in their Monograph No 3 dealing with Waterloo in 1900, draw attention to the LSWR Stevens' pattern 'drop-flap' shunt signal controlling access to Road 5 in the Central Station. In the main print this is just visible between the railings of the low platform on the connecting line. Fortunately the clarity of the print allows for the rather cruel enlargement seen here.

Right: - Another cruel enlargement, but well worth it for the cast advertising plate. The same information was displayed on the right hand column. (...Well you have to get your money's worth for the repro fees for commercial views....)

Hulton Archive / Getty Images 3348023.

WATERLOO

In researching Waterloo for information to accompany the associated photographs two quotes in particular come to mind. The first is from O S Nock in his 1965 book *"The London & South Western Railway"*, in which he describes the old Waterloo as '...a sprawling heterogeneous collection of platforms of all lengths and widths…"

He continued, "While at some time the South Eastern and Brighton railways may have taken the palm for chaotic working of their traffic out on the line, Waterloo, by common consent, was one of the worst examples of terminal working to be found anywhere. Worse was to come later for when Euston was enlarged in 1892, and the temporary arrangements outside the station led to much confusion among passengers arriving by cab, or private carriage, an enraged director said to an operating man, 'You've turned Euston into a Waterloo'".

The final quote by Nock is perhaps slightly better known, but at a time when railway history was characterised by its traditional non-critical writing style, his description of the connection linking the South Western and South Eastern lines was one which perhaps displayed a true sense of personal feeling. "Outside what had originally been designed as a classical frontage, crowned with a handsome portico, looked most odd with the covered way of the single tracked bridge to the South Eastern Railway emerging from that impressive frontage – like a horizontal jet of water from the mouth of a gargoyle". – see illustration opposite.

In reality concessions towards aesthetics may not have been highest in the minds of the South Western directors, although the undoubted confusion that existed in the operation of the terminus had by 1900, already been identified as a major issue to be resolved at some stage.

The original station at Waterloo, part of the site of which had once been a cow shed, had opened in 1848 – a replacement of course for the terminus at Nine Elms, and yet just sixteen years later in 1864, was reported to be handling 200 trains a day. This was accomplished with no interlocking of any sort and with just one signal to stop incoming trains on Westminster Bridge if they could not at that moment be accommodated at the station. Expansion also quickly followed; the 'South Station', also known as 'Cyprus' opened in 1878 – the 'Cyprus' name taken from contemporary events which had seen the British Empire annex the island of the same name. 'North Station', which dated from 1885, was also dubbed 'Khartoum' after the Sudanese campaign of the same year.

The comment at the start of this article about comparing Euston with Waterloo was no doubt also correct, as over the years three distinct stations had evolved (completely excluding the Necropolis

platforms), and which had understandably resulted in daily chaos and confusion. "We got to Waterloo at eleven and asked where the eleven-five started from. Of course nobody knew; nobody at Waterloo ever does know where a train is going to start from, or where a train when it does start is going to, or anything about it.' (*Jerome K Jerome – "Three Men in a Boat"*.)

As an aside for a moment, Waterloo was also unique amongst the various London termini in not

41

Progressing of signalling at Waterloo. '1' is 'A' Box in 1867 - the Necropolis Terminus is behind the wall on the right, next the extended 'A' box in 1878. After that comes the rebuilt 'A' box in 1897 and finally at the bottom of the page, 'A' box in seen in 1922 after what had been a major expansion of signalling two years earlier..

The extremely tall signals associated with the 1878 period were intended to be visible from a great distance - as indeed they would be in clear weather. In conditions of fog however, and with the indication not repeated in any fashion, a train could be halted underneath and have no way of knowing if the signal had cleared. Similarly it was reported that in such weather conditions a signalman could pass a whole shift hearing but not seeing trains passing below.

At '2' the same box seen in 1878 - it was further rebuilt in 1892 and by then contained 266 levers and 21 electric slides for operating route indicating signals. It was commented that there were some 24,000 lever movements every 24 hours - some levers 'double-acting' (presumably standard LSWR 'push-pull' type?), and controlled by six signalman per day shift. Track-circuiting was provided on all routes and there were now route-indicators on the 'A' box home signals. The approaches to the station were controlled by 'B' Box further out towards Vauxhall and which had 100 levers, whilst there was also a 'C' box - visible under the gantry in the third view, with just 30 levers. A suggestion was made in 1910 / 11 for electric signalling to be installed at the but in the event this would have to wait for another 25 years.

'3' a further rebuild in 1907. The six triple bracket signals mounted on top of the gantry in the 1897 view were a particular landmark and not just to train crews. Indeed it was commented that at the time of their removal they would be sorely missed. The box was on two floors, the upper storey containing the lever frame and also a mess room, the lower storey contained the interlocking.

'4' mechanical perfection in 1922 and with a system of gear levers which allowed 72 levers to operate any one of three different signal positions. The first position was for the outgoing starting signal, next the outgoing shunt signal, and the last the incoming shunt position. At this stage there were still eight booking boys and also three telegraph lads, although the latter would soon be replaced with mass installation of telephones.

The signalling at Waterloo was totally modernised with a new electric box from 18th October 1936. This was at the same time as the fly-over at Durnsford Road was brought into use and also complete resignalling between Waterloo and Hampton Court Junction. Such was the planning of the work that on change-over day, the 00.35 am to Hampton Court left under semaphore control, whilst less than an hour later, the 01.30 am to the West of England departed with colour lights.

Rod Garner Collection.

having a station hotel. That is not to say one had not been proposed at some point; not it must be said by the railway company, but instead by a private syndicate which, during the period 1898-1901, proposed 'The South Western Grand Hotel' to be built near the junction of Waterloo Road and York Road and linked to the station by a covered way.

The 1899 August Bank Holiday witnessed 1,049 train movements at the terminus and which was taken as close to capacity. But this was a fact already known to the Board as two years earlier on 9th December 1897, Archibald Scott, a former LSWR General Manager, (General Manager from 1870 to 1885 and now a Director) suggested an extension of the station on the south side over what was considered to be a squalid and overcrowded property area. Indeed it was also around this time that J W Jacomb-Hood, who became Chief Engineer in 1901, paid a visit to America to view the design and operation of several large terminal stations near the east coast.

'The Times' also joined in the criticism on occasions, commenting in an editorial of August 1899 that, "…the cab yard for example was reached by an evil smelling tunnel from York Street." It continued with further comment that the platform congestion was a danger to the public.

Clearly the LSWR could not avoid action for much longer and the company sought powers in a Bill of 1898 to obtain 6.5 acres of land on the south side of the site. The same year must also have been seen some fascinating board meetings, as it appears every meeting included examining plans – and models - of proposed rebuilding schemes, although each it appears was sent back for alteration. (Over a century later one is tempted to ask what might have happened to those various models….?)

However, one conclusion may be gleaned from this and subsequent action; these plans and models referred to the modification of the existing facilities in various forms as they stood. In the end none of the options was deemed suitable and on 21st July 1898 the momentous decision was taken that a total rebuilding of Waterloo was the only realistic option. This was followed by the establishment of a special committee whose sole task was to draw up plans and prepare for a new Parliamentary Bill, and which was rewarded with Royal Assent being granted in 1899.

Even so there had been and was still considerable opposition to overcome, with the London County Council, Lambeth Vestry and Church Authorities all venting their objections. As far as the Council was concerned it was placated by a contribution towards road improvements in the area, whilst the Church alone appeared to speak on behalf of some 1,750 persons whose homes would be due for demolition in what was a squalid and densely populated area.

The human cost in terms of upheaval though was to prove indirectly beneficial. Booth's Poverty Map for the area refers to the location, particularly in the district of the proposed south side extensions, as populated by those in social classes 'Light Blue', through 'Purple', 'Dark Blue', and 'Black', and which for those perhaps unfamiliar with what is a classic reference to the socio-economic situation at the end of the 19th century, identified areas as being 'Poor – 18s. - 21s. a week for a moderate family', through 'Mixed – some comfortable, some poor', 'Very poor – chronic want', to finally, 'Lowest class – vicious semi-criminal'.

The final obstacle to any change at the Terminus was from the London Necropolis Company which had been present since 1854; however, this was also resolved. (See 'The Brookwood Necropolis Railway" by John M Clarke, published by The Oakwood Press).

As would be expected, the first task in rebuilding was site clearance, which meant the numerous residents of the area of proposed expansion were the first to be dealt with. The new powers allowed for the acquisition of 6.5 acres on the south side and the demolition of property in a total of seven streets as well as the Parish Church of All Saints, Lower Marsh, and the associated All Saints School.

Accordingly the LSWR erected a total of six huge blocks of flats, some of these went up in what was then called Boniface Street off Westminster Bridge Road and behind the Bakerloo line tube station, they were ready for occupation in September 1901. Further residential building took place on what would nowadays be deemed a 'brown-field site', this was the former Maudsley Engineering Works, purchased by the LSWR in September 1899.

In total six blocks were build and provided accommodation for 1,750. The work was completed in stages between June 1902 and May 1904. The blocks were also named 'Stangate Buildings' and also 'Campbell Buildings'. The latter after Lieutenant.-Colonel The Honourable. H W Campbell, company chairman from 1899-1904. (There is some slight confusion in the records over the number of blocks at each location, whilst some contemporary commentators have referred to the Lower Marsh area as being occupied by 'Cockneys' - not perhaps strictly true. What is certain is that the LSWR provided more accommodation than was required for on a straight forward replacement basis compared with the demolished property.)

Amongst the property that was demolished were a number of disorderly houses regularly frequented by soldiers and sailors and which had given the area the unfortunate name 'Whoretaloo' – with due respect to

Waterloo - the old and recorded from the 'A' signal box circa 1900.

The confusion of the old station is typified here, and which appears bad enough for the operating department let alone the travelling public. Indeed viewed from this angle it is easy to see how the comparison was drawn with Euston. This conglomeration of tracks had been fed, until 1886, from just four approach / departure lines crossing Westminster Bridge. Two more were added between that date and 1892, a further one making seven in 1900, as would have been the situation here, and finally one extra track making eight in 1916. At this stage to the old Waterloo had 18 platform faces although the confusion often came where a single platform either side of which might boast a platform, played host to just one number. It was according to Henry Wheatley, "Probably the most perplexing station in London'. A fact not lost on the mind of a simple Devon Farmer who after several unsuccessful attempts to find his train is reported to have commented to his wife, "No wonder the French got licked here". A study of the track itself reveals a number of interesting features, the multitude of check rails, the sharp turnouts and the ballast covering and the numerous fouling bars. The various platform widths are also of interest, the platforms, certainly nearest the camera dressed with cross timber. That extending towards the signal box is Platform 8. The signals are also of interest, as under a glass the home signals allowing trains into the various platforms also have their respective platform number painted on them. The two engines just left of centre and facing the camera could well be 'O2' tanks. The one on the right is taking water and appears to have the headcode for a service to Kensington via Richmond, whilst to the right the two discs on the second engine could refers to any one of three different services.

KR Collection / via Mike Thorp

Movement of Light Engines at Waterloo.

Drivers of Light Engines following Passenger Trains out of the Platform Roads at Waterloo Station are instructed, in the event of the Signal at the end of the Platform being at Danger, in all cases to bring their Engines to a stand on the fouling bar situated the platform side of the Signal.

When a Light Engine follows a Train from any Platform Road it should do so very slowly and be under perfect control, in order that it may be stopped immediately should a Hand Signal be shown, or the Train it is following have to slacken speed from any cause, or stop at the Advanced Starting Signal on Westminster Road Signal Bridge.

The Light Engine must not be started until the last vehicle of the departing Train is at least 60 yards ahead, and this space must not be diminished, unless in exceptional circumstances the Engine is required to assist an out-going Train as far as the Starting Signal, when the Driver must comply with the instructions of the Traffic Inspector.

Light Engines must be moved slowly out of the Yard, and the Whistle sounded when necessary for the protection of the staff, or in cases of emergency. Enginemen must keep a good look-out and be prepared to stop if required to do so.

Great caution must be exercised by Drivers of Light Engines in Shunting, or running into or out of any of the Roads, including the Turntable Roads, and on seeing a Hand Signal exhibited they must not move their Engines until they are satisfied that the Hand Signal is intended for them.

The Yard Foreman and Ground Signalman will be held responsible for acting in concert with the Signalman in the " A " Box in giving such Hand Signals.

Drivers of Light Engines when working to the Fixed Signals must not bring their Engines to a stand under the " A " Box, but must stop in such a position as to be within view of the Signalman in the Signal Box.

(LSWR Appendix to the Book of Rules and Regulations. 1st January 1911)

Rebuilding Platforms, etc.

Arched foundations and steelwork for New Entrance

Work below and above ground for the New Memorial Arch

Michael Sadler in his book "Forlorn Sunset". Compensation, but without the same type of entertainment came with the new Union Jack Club which opened in Waterloo Road in 1907.

Finally it might be mentioned that the former parish of All Saints was incorporated by cordial arrangement into that of St Johns in Waterloo Road. No mention though is made of a replacement or amalgamation in so far as the school was concerned. Despite offers – possibly from the LCC to manage the new estate, the LSWR decided to retain control, achieving a net rental return of 2.75%. The total cost of the new residential construction, and presumably land purchase was £255,802 whilst it should also be mentioned that all the blocks referred to have long been demolished. (There was also a Campbell Road in Eastleigh provided around the same time, again probably from the same origins.) .

With the residential area cleared, it was necessary to dig between 15 and 25 feet down into either hard gravel or in some cases London clay in order to find a secure footing. Indeed water was encountered in considerable volume with a tributary of the Thames still flowing underground beneath the station – hence also the nearby road of Lower Marsh. Despite the work there were very few claims for disturbance caused by almost continuous pumping operations. A number of arches were altered or extended or provided, some of these rented out as workshops and wine cellars.

From a railway perspective the first tangible change was the re-siting of the Necropolis station in 1902 although at track level it would still be some time before actual platform and concourse alterations would be effected. J W Jacomb-Hood would also oversee most of the rebuilding period, although after his accidental death in March 1914 – he fell from his horse whilst hunting at Dulverton, work was under control of the new Chief Engineer A W Szlumper. Resident Engineer was R D Hawes.

The original rebuilding plans had been for no less than a 24 road terminus and at a total cost of £900,000. It would also appear, and possibly following the experience of Jacomb-Hood in America, that a straight line end to all the platforms was preferable although local space constraints would preclude that aspect. The 24 platform terminus was also quickly reduced to 23 faces and then, following the later experience with the new suburban electric sets and their ability to affect a fast platform turnaround, to 21 platforms. Interestingly Platform 1 was for some time intended to be reserved for Royal and VIP traffic only, and for which purpose an adjacent doorway enabled

'The Great and The Good' to arrive and depart surreptitiously if required.

It was essential also that whilst the rebuilding work was taking place, the station could still function as normally as possible, and it was the proud boast of the LSWR later that throughout the eventual 20 plus years rebuilding programme no train was held up nor passenger injured in consequence. Indeed there is only incident referred to during the period (surely there must have been more…?), which took place on 5th May 1904 when a signal linesman involved in routine maintenance trod on a signal wire which was sufficient to clear the indication for a milk train to depart. Unfortunately this occurred just as another train was arriving, with the result that one passenger was killed.

At the same time as work on the terminus was taking place, powers were obtained in 1898 and 1902 allowed for the widening of approach tracks, so that by 1916 there were eight lines leading to and from the station. This though might not have been the limit, as the same powers had allowed the company to purchase sufficient to lay a total of 11 lines if required.

Few beneficial changes would have been noticed by travellers before about 1909, as the years 1900 through to 1910 had been mainly involved in dealing with the sub-structure, the marsh area and the strengthening of the existing arches. At the same time, by 1906, steel was being delivered on a regular basis although it was reported that in the same year these deliveries had fallen behind schedule.

Eventually though work had advanced sufficiently for the 'new' south station to be completed as far as Platform 4 by 25th September 1909, and which also enabled the new facilities to be available for the Territorial Army Manoeuvres of the same year. Platform 5 was next, and was brought into use on 6th March 1910. The new platforms were likewise used for the funeral of King Edward V11 in the same year as well as travel arrangements in connection with the Coronation of the new King, George V, in 1911. Interestingly the roofing over the concourse was the subject of separate contracts and construction did not apparently proceed at the same rate; this was a feature of the work throughout the rebuilding. A note in the records reveals that to allow for re-roofing to take place, Platforms 2 and 3 would be temporarily taken out of use on 3rd July 1911 and a temporary wooden gangway provided to connect Platform 1 directly with Platform 4.

The main office block behind the concourse was approved by the Board on 7th January 1909 and completed on 7th November 1910. To start with lighting and heating was obtained from the power station of the

Opposite page: - Extract from the Volume V111 No 85, of the 'South Western Railway Magazine' for April 1922, and as referred to in the main text.
Rod Garner Collection.

nearby Waterloo & City railway although from 1915 this came direct from Durnsford Road. (The Waterloo & City had opened in 1898.)

This office block would also eventually incorporate various facilities for the comfort of passengers including a 'Gentleman's Basement Lavatory' described by the Railway Magazine as, "… perhaps the finest in England". Perhaps a slightly less gender specific use came from the new Booking Hall which opened on 11th June 1911.

It is now necessary to move away from the practicalities and back to the boardroom and the arrival of a new Chairman, Brigadier-General Sir Hugh Drummond, Bart. in 1911. According to Faulkner & Williams ("*The LSWR in the Twentieth Century*"), the new appointment "…brought more decision…", and which therefore must imply that perhaps the impetus had waned slightly over the past years. Perhaps an even more positive move forward was when Sir Herbert Walker was appointed General Manager the following year, although destiny would play its part in not helping what was still a mammoth project be completed during the years of hostility that would follow. (See Chronology of Reconstruction on Page 53.)

With a project of such magnitude there were also bound to be design changes along the way commensurate with altering traffic demands. Previous to Drummond's tenure, each stage of the work had been the subject of board discussion and consequential delay, but it appears now the General Manager was permitted a much more 'hands-on' approach whilst Drummond determined the work should be completed as soon as possible.

As will be gathered, work was progressing basically on an east to west basis across the station and with the 'Central' station ready to be dealt with next. Accordingly the decision was taken to abandon the former connection with the SECR. This was taken out of use on 26th March 1911 although the pedestrian footbridge linking the two stations was retained. The cab approaches to the main line platforms were also closed from 1st January 1912.

The new management certainly appears to have made matters move apace, as from June 1912 to the summer of 1913 the old offices alongside Platform 1 were taken down and their occupants moved either to the completed section of the new office block or to temporary accommodation off York Road. Some also went to other temporary accommodation in the vacated offices of the Locomotive department at Nine Elms.

Under his own leadership, Sir Herbert Walker also had progress in mind and in July 1912 he was able to report that the Engineering Committee had set out both a programme for, and estimated cost for, the remaining works:

1 – Completion of Platforms 6-11 and the central cab yard £75,000.
2 – Completion of new roofing and a screen to connect with the old north station £79,000.
3 – Further office buildings (extension 2) with concourse roofing. Completion of Waterloo Road cab yard and subway to concourse £75,000.
4 – Completion of platforms working from the north £71,000.

It would seem that at this stage the original plans were still for a total of ten Windsor Line platforms, but coupled with a decline in inner suburban traffic (still steam worked at this stage) and the fact that the 1885 station roof was in good condition, the result was a saving in expenditure and a more spacious, less congested, Windsor Line concourse.

Board approval was quickly given on 26th July 1912, and with the additional note that the General Manager and Chief Engineer were to decide the order of priorities. Clearly the decision had also been made to use an obvious simple consecutive platform numbering system, as from 1st December 1912, the South, Central and North stations were no longer referred to as such and instead there was a simple numerical system. Starting from the south the existing old platforms became numbers 6 through to 17, following on from those already in use in what was the new south station. (Numbers 6 to 11 came into use in 1913). A further guide as to progress is that by the summer of 1913 eight out of the eventual 21 platforms were completed and in service, whilst early in 1914 that figure had passed the half way mark with eleven now in use. Keeping with the 'platform' topic for a moment, it should be mentioned that Platform 21 would eventually be used for milk traffic.

Meanwhile around 1912-1913, a new stairway was provided from Waterloo Road to the concourse together with a subway to the Waterloo & City and Bakerloo Lines.

Sir Hugh Drummond made a formal tour of the work on 22nd April 1913 and at which time the new steel

Another classic view from the Hulton Archive / Getty Images collection. This time the photograph was taken on 30th September 1919, still during the strike period and with the terminus seemingly conspicuously silent. At the bottom of each signal post can be Stevens type 'Bow-Tie' or 'scissor' arms and controlling wrong-road working.

Hulton Archive / Getty Images 3163846

The new entrance through the 28 feet Victory Arch, or Memorial Arch, as it was sometimes known. The view was taken during the opening ceremony on Tuesday 21st March 1922. It was reported later that the Arch was a particularly draughty thoroughfare so perhaps it was just as well King George V did not attend on the day. The importance the populace displayed at the time in attempting to gain a view of proceedings will be noted by the group on the ladder. The carvings on either side represented war and peace. Within the platforms were built 20 feet above street level.
Rod Garner Collection

roof was complete as far as what would later be Platform 11. The new Refreshment and Dining Rooms were also almost ready at this stage – these were subsequently opened on 27th June 1913 although the railway company was not responsible for the catering which instead lay in the hands of the firm - Spiers & Pond.[1]

By June 1913 sections 1-3 of the July 1912 schedule were almost complete and on 29th January 1914 work was authorised to start on Platforms 12 to15. There was though a delay on the office block which, although authorised back on 26th June 1913, was reported as being held up by a builders' strike in February 1914.

Meanwhile the old roof of the former Central Station had been propped up and steelwork for the new roof erected around it. Some of the old roof was removed in the year 1912-1913 although the last fragments were not taken down until 29th November 1915.

A general note in the files now refers to, "Work planned in 1913, suspended during war time until armistice". Possibly this refers to Section 4 of the July 1912 schedule and in which case Waterloo must have appeared somewhat piecemeal during the ensuing years. Even so some work did continue although progress was understandably slower.

Indeed reports for the years 1914-1915 indicate work being undertaken on the central cab road between Platforms 11 and 12, whilst Platforms 15 to17 were taken out of use for reconstruction in concrete in 1914-1915 and had their track realigned during 1915-17.

Opposite page: - 'Waterloo New Station' from the South Western Railway Magazine. According to the Magazine, the concourse was the principal feature of the new station and having a total length of 760 feet. Within the main offices staff have access to, "...a spacious dining room with up to date kitchen. In charge as Station Master at the time of the formal opening was Mr Jerrett.
Rod Garner Collection

Views of Concourse from North (Windsor Line) side.

Views of Concourse from South (Main Line) side.

Section of Main Line Departure Platform.   View showing Special Construction of Station Roof.

WATERLOO - THE STATISTICS

Between 1900 and 1921 and including the peaks during the war years, five million trains were handled at Waterloo and a total of 750 million passengers.

In 1922 the station dealt with between 1,159 and 1,200 trains every 24 hours, and reaching 1,370 on occasions.

140,000 passengers used the station every day. Of these 326 were steam and 126 parcels, milk, or empty stock. The average daily total in 1906 was 692 trains daily.

The floodlit 'Victory Arch'. "This modern method of spectacular lighting is especially suited to buildings having an ornamental façade and decorative features, which are thrown into striking relief by flooding the stonework with light from concealed lamps. In the particular case there was some difficulty in finding a suitable spot from which to project the light, but eventually two special diffusive searchlights of 1,600 candle power each were placed on the granite pedestals, later to be occupied by ornamental lanterns. From these points the greater part of the light was distributed, two small supplementary projectors being used higher up on each side."

Rod Garner Collection

(Does this mean they were out of use until re-alignment?) They were reported as ready for the commencement of electric services in October 1915.

Just before this in June 1915, Board authority had been given for all the remaining work to be completed. Even so progress was understandably slow, due both to labour and materials shortage and the prevailing economic situation. Accordingly two years later in October 1917, the Engineering Committee estimated work to the value of £210,000 still remained to be completed. (It is difficult to be accurate with regard to costs, mainly due to the effect of inflation during both WW1 and what was a period of protracted building. What can be said is that the original 19th century estimate of £900,000 had risen to £2,269,354 by 1922 and out of which £567,857 was accountable to the purchase of land.)

Despite the difficult situation prevailing the LSWR were at the same time clearly looking ahead. An escalator was purchased from the OTIS Company in New York in 1915 and safely moved across the Atlantic for eventual use between Platforms 15 and 16 and the Waterloo & City. It would not be in use though until 9th April 1919. Additionally Platforms 1 -15 each had a short flight of steps midway giving access to the tube lines. Parcels – the parcels department was underneath the main station - were dealt with by another subway and lifts and so avoided the need for trolleys on the concourse.

One fact widely quoted afterwards was the volume of meals served at the 'Waterloo Station Free Buffet for Soldiers and Sailors' and staffed entirely by female volunteers. This was located in the subway and dispensed in the order of 3,000 meals daily together with an estimated 18 million cups of tea in the years between 1915 and 1920. (The opening date for the 'Free Buffet' varies according to which reference is used, and is quoted as either 19th December 1915 or 6th January 1916. Closure was on 7th April 1920.)

It is not believed the final section of the new work, of dealing with the former 'North' station was commenced until around 1920, previous on-site examination having also shown that the existing columns here, dating from 1885, were in good condition thus allowing for a saving in expenditure. Accordingly the 'North' station roof supports were retained although with the new roofing fitted this meant that for decades there was a slight variation in height and slightly above 60 feet. Most travellers and a good proportion of the staff probably never noticed.

Consequently there was now available a space between Platforms 15 and 16 for a two storey office block that came to be known as 'The Village'. This work was completed by the LSWR's own staff and was ready for occupation from 14th December 1919. It tended to be used more by the actual Waterloo staff, rather than Headquarters staff, and included the offices of the Station Master. The total station staff was for many years in the order of 450. The same year saw the contract placed for the new roof over the Windsor Line Platforms and also the cab road at the front of the station.

A suburban lines booking office opposite Platforms 14 and 15 opened on 22nd July 1918 which meant the old Windsor Line Booking Office could be demolished. The contractors, Messrs Perry & Co could also then proceed with the completion of the main office block on the concourse, steel framed within but outside of mellow brick with Portland stone ornamentation. The Main Booking Hall, with access from the front roadway, dealt with the issue of longer distance tickets.

As a safety measure, each platform had at its end a set of massive hydraulic buffers having a seven foot stroke and capable of arresting a 400 ton train travelling at 10 mph.

TO BE CONTINUED.IN
THE JANUARY 2008 ISSUE

The famous clock. This was installed in in 1919 and could at last counter the claim in 'Punch' that previously all the clocks at the station kept different time!

The new clocks were proudly reported as 'all-electric" and similarly all synchronised. Commentators noted that each face seemingly had no mechanism whilst practically the 'workings' for each face would almost be carried in an overcoat pocket.

This of course was located on the concourse and was the location for countless thousands of 'meetings under the clock'.

Interestingly even then the use of the 24-hour designation will be noted.

Rod Garner Collection

'T14' No 460 as rebuilt by Maunsell in April 1930. The train is a Portsmouth express running via Cosham. Following rebuilding, Waterloo station occupied a total of some 24.5 acres, 10 acres of which were roofed. The roofed area was also fan-shaped and with specially designed ventilation which allowed smoke and steam to through special openings. As such Waterloo never suffered the grime associated with a number of other terminal stations.

Dave Hammersley Collection

NEW STOCK FOR THE EASTLEIGH BREAKDOWN TRAIN - 1957

As replacements for earlier stock, two former LSWR 57 foot 'Ironclad' vehicles were refitted for use with the Eastleigh Breakdown crane in 1957.

Furthest from the camera is Tool Van No DS175, a former 3rd class coach dating from July 1921 and originally LSWR No 774, later SR No 718. The Riding Vehicle (Coach No 1) is DS172, a former Pantry 3rd, built at the same time and formerly LSWR No 930, SR No 713. This particular coach was once part of a five-car Bournemouth line set. In external appearance the van was now not dissimilar to the earlier style of Mail Vans minus of course the panelling. The position of the former windows though is readily apparent.

The conversions were no doubt carried out at Eastleigh and were recorded here by the official photographer on 18th June 1957. Livery would have been bright red. Interestingly the steam heat-facilities appear to have been removed whilst although the number of doors now available have obviously been restricted, no additional grab handles affording access from ground level have been added.

Inside DS175 is a veritable plethora of equipment, the exact contents built up over a century of experience. This was also referred to as 'Coach No 2 Tools and Appliances for Re-railing'. Amongst the items that can be made out are obvious packing, jacks and what are probably acetylene lamps. There are also two gas-cylinders at the far end as well as the obvious 'No Smoking' sign that goes with them. On the coach side is also a derrick for swinging the heavy jacks out onto ground level - did the coach structure have to be strengthened to accommodate this?

This page, top left: - 'Coach No 1' the cooking range and water heater. The water supply was from an extended roof tank. Coal fuel was obviously not a problem! But just notice that asbestos lagging.

Top right: - 'Staff Dining and Rest Compartment' and compared with the lower view which is 'Compartment for use of Officers', the polished table in the latter will be noted although the upholstery is of the same moquette.

Opposite page top: - DS35 is a Ransomes & Rapier 36 ton crane dating from 1918. This particular vehicle was allocated to Nine Elms until 1937, then Fratton, and finally Eastleigh from 1946. It was withdrawn in 1964.

Opposite page, lower: - Finally underneath DS172, the opportunity was taken to locate even more hawsers and tackle. This feature was common to both vehicles and ran across the whole width of the under frames being accessed from either side.

Above: The South Eastern and Chatham Railway was hardly renowned for the comfort of it's rolling stock, in fact quite the reverse. However in 1913 work was started on the design of a new and improved Continental Boat Train, but it was not until 1921 that the first train designed by Maunsell and Lynes was delivered. To a new and quite luxurious standard, these 62ft long corridor vehicles presented quite a different appearance with match-boarded lower sides and inward opening doors at the ends of the coach, similar to the Pullman stock with which they were designed to run. Further vehicles were subsequently built to slightly differing designs and width. Here we see the corridor side of Restriction 1 'Continental' 3rd S 1007 S in BR Crimson and Cream livery at the rear of a train at Headcorn on 13th May 1953. This coach was built by the Birmingham Railway Carriage and Wagon Co in 1924 as 2nd class coach 4179 with seven compartments and a coupe to Diagram 935. It was downrated to 3rd and renumbered in 1934. The 'bend' in the handrail on the right hand side of the door and the absence of a rail on the left indicates that the doors have been altered to open outwards. The coach was withdrawn by 1961.

Opposite page - top: Whilst the SECR was designing its Boat train stock the LSWR was also building new corridor trains which differed markedly from previous designs. Designed by Surrey Warner the first of these 57ft vehicles were ordered in 1915. The coaches became known as 'Ironclads', by virtue of their robust appearance and steel sheeting instead of wooden paneling. Here is corridor all 1st No 7181 built at Eastleigh in 1922 to Diagram 476 in Southern Green livery at Clapham Junction next to newly built Bulleid Brake 4366 on an empty stock train, 21st April 1948.. Many of the Ironclads had Warner 'Dreadnought' bogies as is the case here. Now running as a 'loose' coach, 7181 which had 42 first class seats was initially formed into one of the Southampton Boat train traffic sets. A considerable number of Ironclad coaches were built not only for Boat traffic but also for Bournemouth and West of England services. 7181 was withdrawn in January 1959.

Opposite page - lower: And now for something completely different. The SECR purchased eight steam railmotors in the early 1900s These proved not to be a great success and were all taken out of service after a few years service and stored. In 1924 the Southern Railway rebuilt four of them into a two pairs of articulated two-coach sets, Nos 513 and 514 for branch line work. They were not Push-Pull fitted unlike the other four railmotors which were rebuilt as two similar although non-articulated sets. The pair seen were sent to the Sheppey Light Railway until that closed in 1951. By June 1952 set 513 had migrated to the Hayling Island branch and it is seen here in the bay platform at Hayling Island on 18th June 1952. It carries BR Crimson Livery and its appearance suggests that it has only recently been outshopped. The set comprises 3rd Brake 3560 and 3rd 975 and is 100ft long, rated at 45 ton, providing 121 3rd class seats and is Restriction 1. These two sets were the only articulated coaches ever to run on the Southern Railway.

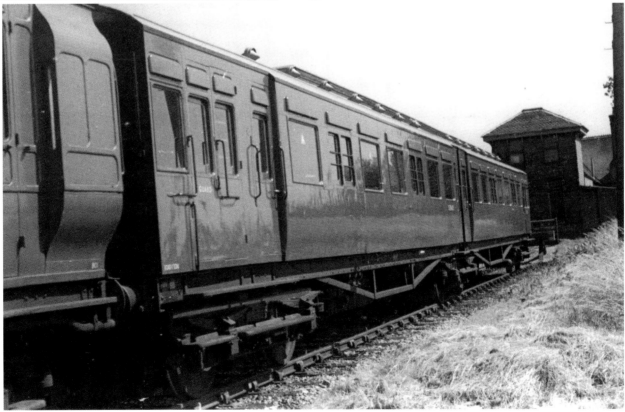

PERMANENT WAY NOTES

by Graham Hatton

So how do move a train of 360 feet lengths of track from Basingstoke to Woking...?

... like this of course.

Left: - Basingstoke Up West Yard July 1952. The first of a series of official photographs to show a Long Welded Rail Train (LWRT) undergoing a series of apparently staged movements.

The train has arrived in the yard on the Up Reception line off the Up Slow at Winklebury. It's carrying two groups of consecutive lengths of 360ft conductor rail and careful location paint marks have been painted on the bolsters. The rails are chained to each wagon to hold their central location which also restricted their longitudinal movement slightly. (Modern rail trains have the rail clamped centrally only allowing some controlled movement in the direction of the train on curves with guides to allow greater freedom of movement).

Of interest in the photograph also is the former Alton Line curving away to the left before the houses. This line also served the Thorneycroft Factory and continued to do so after closure of the through route, adopting that name as the siding name. The stub end of this line is still there, curving away into the bushes! To the right of the photo was known as the Wash Out Siding and to the right of this behind the lighting poles is the Park Prewett Branch which served the nearby large psychiatric hospital. It curved away to the right just beyond the sidings following the route of what is now a dual carriageway to the extensive hospital grounds. All the sidings visible in this photograph were still in place, though out of use, in 2006, but the majority have been removed with the re-signalling in progress in 2007.

Right: - The train has moved forward in this picture and is photographed straddling a BH 'C' switch to 1:10 crossing crossover including a tandem turnout (for the technically minded!). Many turnouts in sidings were the tighter 'B'switches to 1:8 crossings but the view shows how the rail flexed to follow the underlying track. This flexing caused some longitudinal movement in the rails. Speed over such routes was always very slow, but rail, particularly the softer conductor rail, flexes reasonably easily. In the view in front of the train is Basingstoke steam shed, the station is in the middle to the left of the home signals and the Down West Yard including the water tower and main line signal box are on the right. The rail wagons appear to have different tops and this shows the rather unplanned composition of these trains from often adapted chassis.

Delivery of rail in long lengths considerably reduces the needs of site welding and over the years different lengths have been trialled up to about 900ft. However, most rail now is delivered in 600ft lengths on modern purpose built trains. Many earlier rail trains used old coach underframes suitably modified. Trains like this were still in use in the 1980s. The final wagon was a 'shoot' wagon which had a metal rail shoot on its rear. A clamp was fitted to the running rail behind the train on site and a wire rope stretched through the shoot rollers and clamped to the relevant rail on the LWRT. It was then a matter of drawing the train forward as each rail was pulled off the back until finally dropping to the ground off the shoot wagon in a fairly dramatic style! This process carried on with little change into the 1980s, but Health & Safety and a concern over rail damage has led to more controlled methods of unloading and lowering rail from purpose built trains. Some new trains are able to reload rail from the ground, something not possible with the train in the view which had to be loaded at a rail loading yard capable of lifting and slewing the rail onto the train in one go.

Above: The train has moved forward still further and it's clear how the rail has formed a curve to more or less follow the track beneath the train, though by their nature the wagons have a more angular shape. It appears to have generated some interest amongst the adjacent staff as it snakes out of the yard onto the Up Slow.

Slip switches, on the exit from the yard to the main line, are usually tighter radius because of their restricted geometry, so there must have been some interest here in the rail movement, not to mention some interesting noises from the rails!

To the left are Basingstoke loco sheds, no doubt along with many loco sheds containing some 'challenging track'!

Between the LWRT loco and the shed area is a single line which ran from the Up Reception round the outside of the SW station linking into the Reading GW line via their old station site. It was removed and the Up side station entrance altered some years ago, but its reinstatement due to the increasing freight use of this line is periodically suggested.

Of course the train must have been formed elsewhere and run to Basingstoke as there are no rail welding or loading facilities here, but the presence of an official photographer and paint markings does suggest this was some form of trial run. The photos are marked up as 'special train Basingstoke to Woking'. Although not possible to identify the exact machine we do know the loco at the head was an unrebuilt Bulleid Pacific.

Top right: The train has moved now to Woking Up Yard and is believed to be setting back into the yard. In a similar view to that at Basingstoke it shows how the rail flexes to follow the underlying track, here it's a series of crossovers.

The exit from the Up Yard has changed little today and the signal box, so typical of Southern Boxes built at this time, remains.

A buffer stop has also been placed on the left siding end nowadays; the lack of one in the photograph suggests there may have been a minor incident here! The view also contains a good range of period vehicles in the adjacent road, and although much has been rebuilt in Woking almost all the railway and external buildings in this view remain today.

Lower right - *Caption overleaf.*

Previous page -lower:: - The train has now set back into the P.Way Yard at Woking (on the Up side.). This appears to be a tighter curve and it shows how the rail curved on the wagons and has now been forced sideways on the second wagon in the view when the paint marks on the wagon floor are viewed. It is just possible to make out the break between the lengths of LWR near the raised crane jib. Propelling a relatively 'stiff 'train like this was something attempted with due respect! Of interest also in the yard are the typical P.Way cranes of the day rated typically at up to 15 tons capacity. For most P.Way work this was adequate. During the week the cranes would form up components, load engineer's wagons and build up new track layouts such as that behind the first crane on the left. After building up, if the pointwork was to be laid locally, it might be broken into large pieces and transferred to site as an 'out of gauge load'. If it was to travel further, then the running rails were usually replaced with scrap rail and the layout 'burnt' into portions of three timbers or about 7'6" in length, for loading onto wagons (timbers parallel with the wagon). The reverse process would happen on site. The portions of track would be laid out in three timber sections to the final line, the burnt short rails removed as scrap and the final rails replaced. Sometimes the layouts were simply painted with location numbers and marks and disassembled for movement to site. Stacks of timbers (the name given to anything longer than a sleeper and usually slightly bigger in section), sleepers, rails, baseplates etc. are laid out to make loading or their use easier. Note the timber handling 'dog' lying on top of the nearest sleeper pile. From this view it's also just possible to make out the underframes of the LWRT wagons.

This page - Waterloo Station (South Side) on 2 June 1954, just after completion of the remodelling of the approach to platforms 1 to 7. Note all the speed restriction commencement boards marked 'C' by the lines affected. Only nowadays is the actual temporary speed restriction speed marked. At this time the driver needed to refer to the weekly operating notices.

'REBUILDING' - THE LETTERS AND COMMENTS PAGE

Two obvious gremlins crept into the 'Preview Issue', the first refers to the site where the trackwork for the relaying at Lewisham was pre-assembled. This should have been stated to be Cold Blow Sidings. I am grateful to Alan Blackburn, amongst others, for this addition.

The final view in the 'Found in a Wooden Box' series of Salisbury also depicts the GWR and not the Southern turntable. Well, we like to appeal to a broader church... Graham Muspratt, was amongst several who pointed this out, thank you for your input. Also to the gentlemen who stated the curtains in the houses opposite were ones he recognised.

Former Eastleigh fitter, Eric Best, contacted us to mention that the source information we had used to refer to the demise of 'Abergavenny' and 'Bessborough' – Don Bradley's books, was in fact incorrect. Eric was one of the men involved in the demise of 'Besborough' and which took place at the top of No 4 bay at Eastleigh – not Brighton.

Finally to Eric Youldon and John Fry. One of the photographs of the motion in the 'Merchant Navy' article was printed back to front when I received it. It appeared in the same form in the Preview Issue. So if you do try building one and all the pieces don't fit together now you know why.

Letters: -

Unfortunately the intended space for readers letters is simply not available whilst space and realism prevent the inclusion of all writings. Even so I acknowledge with grateful thanks correspondence and constructive comments from the following,

Ian Bull, Tony Bush, Howard Butler, Denis Calvert, Colin Chivers, Peter Clarke, Torry Clyde, Irvine Cresswell, Brian Drysdall, Fred Emery, Mike Esau, Richard Foot, Ian Giles, Tony Goodyear, Colin Hall, Philip Hall, Dave Hammersley, Doug Hannah, Natalie Jones, T S Keep, Jeff Langham, John Lewis, Bert Moody Keith Muston, Nigel Overington, Eric Penn, Alan Postlethwaite, Chris Rooney, W S Randell, Colin Reuben, Blair Robinson, Sue Rose, Dennis Tillman, John Wenyon and Mick Wildey

Appeal: – Does anyone have a plan of the various electric car sheds at Littlehampton, Farnham, Worthing, Clapham Junction etc….? No prizes for guessing why.

Finally, thanks to Dave Hammersley, he of 'Roxey Mouldings' fame, for reading the text and Bruce Murray, photographic genius.

The new track layout features a number of modern features at that time, including full depth cast crossings, (see Southern Way Preview Issue). There is a most interesting variation on a scissors crossover to the Down Slow on the left leading from platforms 1, 2 & 3 and a double slip in the mid distance, with the two normally straight crossover lines curved through the turnout in this cramped and angled approach to the station. Note also that the right hand far leg of this unusual, but by no means unique, double slip has a curve to the left extending through the crossing starting at the slip switch toes. Quite a challenging layout to model! The photo comes from an interesting group of photos showing this remodelling and which was recorded at the end of the work with some minor 'fettling' being carried out. (A series of photographs on this relaying at Waterloo will feature in a later issue.) The route indicator appears to have been set from platform 3 suggesting the track to be back in use, though it's possible this could be for signal testing. All the movements at Waterloo were controlled from the very large and solidly built box to the right of the 2 car electric set. These platforms have become the starting point for a large proportion of the local services (along with the Windsor side platforms on the other side of the station). Although the layout appears complex it is largely based on two overlapping fans of tracks from the incoming Up Slow and outgoing tracks to the Down Slow, allowing access to all platforms in this group from 1-7. Further groups of tracks exist and are connected in the Waterloo West Crossing area, just in the far left background, but moves in this group were largely self-contained with the advent of multiple units, thus assisting the free flow of trains in parallel at this busy station. The middle platforms carried outer suburban and longer distance trains in general and the far platforms, where the electric unit is heading to/from, led to the Windsor Side platforms. Waterloo has a most fascinating and complex history which is still evolving. The South Western Circle, the historical society for the LSWR has recently published a most excellent and detailed history of the LSWR's development of Waterloo from conception to the Southern Railway takeover of the system produced by Colin Chivers & Philip Wood. It includes a huge number of good photos and diagrams of the original South Station and the other two almost separate stations on this site which were referred to jointly as Waterloo. The LSWR took the plunge & rebuilt the entire site into the single airy station of today. The original modernisation plans for this redevelopment first appeared in 1899 and it took about 23 years to finish the building work! Details of the society, of interest to anyone with an historical interest in the LSWR, are available on the internet. www.lswr.org

...AND NOW FOR SOMETHING COMPLETELY DIFFERENT...

Bournemouth shed, Saturday 9th June 1956 - and before you ask, no it is not a manipulated or trick view.

Sandwiched between 35010 'Blue Star' and 34008 'Padstow' is 5081 'Lockheed Hudson' which had arrived on a through excursion from Great Malvern.* This would not be the first time a 'Castle was seen in Hampshire as on another occasion a member of the class arrived at Portsmouth and was 'impounded' by the Southern Region at Fratton Shed - stored behind a line of other engines, until some means could be found of getting the interloper away again.

Notwithstanding the fact that on this occasion the various platform edges appeared to have been left intact on the way down, the blanket ban on the 'Castle' class running on the Western Section of the Southern Region was rigidly enforced and the return excursion was hauled by 73112 as far as Reading West. 5081 was sent back light engine, and subject to a 25mph restriction - never to venture south again.

(* According to Special Traffic Notice P.28, S.D., 1956, this was an unadvertised excursion leaving Great Malvern at 6.50 am and arriving on the Southern Region at Basingstoke at 10.01 am. Here there was a wait for 13 minutes after which it was non-stop to Bournemouth Central, apart from a one minute pause at Eastleigh for 'Train Crew Requirements only' - presumably to pick up a Pilotman. Arrival at the destination was scheduled for 11.58 am, after which the stock would leave for the sidings at Bournemouth West. The return working was 7.40 pm from Bournemouth.)

Photo: Mark Abbott

Opposite page: - The original Beddington Lane Signal Box in 1926 and at the station of the same name on the former joint LSWR / LBSCR line from Wimbledon to West Croydon. Opened as far back as 1855, part of the original route in the vicinity of Mitcham was later doubled, although as illustrated here, there also remained an oasis of calm amongst the otherwise frenetic suburban routes of South London.

...OR FOR QUIETER
CONTEMPLATION...

A panoramic view of the works and which can be dated with some accuracy as around July 1946. (The two new West Country Class engines 21C135 and 21C136 assist in this way as they were reported as both 'new to Traffic in the same month.) The view is taken from Howard Place at Brighton and which from its high vantage point was where we did our trainspotting.   *Colin Hall Collection*

Key: 'A'   *Clothing Store*   'E'   *Erecting Shop - East Bay*
        'B'   *Viaduct to Lewes*   'F'   *Boiler Shop*
        'C'   *Compressor House*   'G'   *Weigh House*
        'D'   *Works - West Bay*

The Author - left and fellow apprentice, Allan Attack alongside newly built BR Standard Class 4 tank, No 80137.

BRIGHTON LOCO WORKS

'Apprenticeship Memories'

Brian Newby Potts

In 1952, Brighton Works celebrated its 100 years anniversary and that was also the year I started my five year fitter and turner apprenticeship. I could not have guessed at the time, but at the conclusion of my training I would have spent just one week as a fitter before transferring to the No 1 Design Drawing Office which had also been the objective of serving my apprenticeship in the first place. Quite reasonably, one could not enter into design without experience gained on the works floor.

Apprentice Training School

The first five months was spent under the supervision of Reg Nunn in the Apprenticeship Training School which was located near the Plating Shop and Millwrights. We made a number of tools as well as exercise pieces, including a square bar made from an old bolt, filed and 'miked' up and a spanner which had to fit the square bar perfectly in all directions including when reversed. Similarly, a hexagonal bolt and fitting spanner were also made. After this came a plate with a slot, about 6' long and ½' wide that had a sliding insert which had to move up and down in the slot without being allowed to fall out when fitted both ways. Further tools were also made such as calipers - inside and out, oddlegs, tool makers clamps, surface plates (three off), tap wrenches (2 sizes), and a tri-square. We also made scrapers usually from old files. It was all a great difference to school times, starting at 0730 with an hour off for lunch 1230-1330, then through till 1700. One full day and two nights were spent each week at Technical College.

During the weekdays I was in 'digs', with 'Auntie Mary' at 74 Old Shoreham Road, travelling home to Kingston in Surrey on a Friday night and returning on Sunday night. Unfortunately my parents had moved from Brighton in 1950. 'Auntie Mary' went to Dover after about a year and I obtained new digs in Preston Drove before moving to 56 Warleigh Road with Mrs. Barlow. Despite being away from home I was fortunate in having a friend, David Heathcote, who lived nearby.

My parents later moved to Reigate and so from 1954 onwards I travelled up and down daily, getting up at 0520 and going by bus to Earlswood station, then train to Brighton. There were even times when I would cycle the 30 odd miles each way especially on 'Tech' days.

Fitting Shop

Following the initial spell in the Training School the next step was to the Fitting Shop, under the watch of Les, Foreman of the Motion Gang. This lasted for nearly a year; I was often working with an amiable character who had once been in the Merchant Navy, Don Pleasance.

It was at the Fitting Shop that I first encountered a hydraulic press which stood near one of the benches, and was used to push out the old, and insert new, gunmetal bushes from the rods. Oil rings were also fitted to the bearing bushes, with two half bearings for connecting rod big ends fitted to the openings. Pins and collars with their securing taper pins were also fitted. Once a coupling rod which had just been lapped dropped onto my fingers – blood everywhere! We also fitted die blocks to expansion links.

Testing was a very important aspect which was undertaken on a Magnetic Testing Machine. Here the various rods were first covered in a mixture of metal filings and paraffin, then when the machine was switched on any cracks could be easily identified. In practice it was rare to find any.

Bearings were scraped to a finish fit complete with their pins, the actual motion polished up by draw-filing and finished off with emery paper. Newly made parts had their sharp machined edges and facings gently radiused by hand finishing whilst oil gutters were cut with a round nose chisel and finished with files.

Erecting Shop

I spent two periods in part of the Erecting Shop either side of about nine months working on lathes in what was referred as 'The Turnery'; this was under the charge of 'Ginger' Andrews. Here we made various flanges for sand pipes, facing and boring out the various holes. The trouble was that you got so many to do in a batch that it became rather boring. Some variety came with spring hangers which were also turned, the centre part cut being about ¼', whereas the curved parts at the outer ends were generated and then finished with a large forming tool. The finish had to be very smooth to avoid fractures. Whilst taking one of the deep cuts, a piece of ¼' swarf flew off (and in those days no one except the grinders wore goggles) and hit me in the white of my eye burning into it as well as my cheek. After having this removed at the Eye Hospital and with a pad dressing covering my eye, I spent some weeks in the Drawing

AEROPLANE VIEW OF BRIGHTON L.M.9. RY. WORKS.

Looking south-west across to the works. The conglomeration of New England Road - leading down from the letter 'G'; London Road, Viaduct Road - just out of view at the bottom of the view, and Preston Circus. Access to the works was via New England Street, indicated at 'H'. Just by the arrowhead leading from the letter 'G' is the bridge carrying the lower goods line. Above this were some shops on piers. Some idea of the vast expanse of the works can be gauged from this picture.

Key: 'A' = Millwrights and Welders Shop. 'B' = Copper Smith's Shop. 'C' = Fitting Shop. 'D' = Erecting Shop - and having the taller roof. The east bay of this shop was 600 feet long. 'E' = Machine Shop. 'F' = Tool Room. 'G' = New England Road and leading down to Preston Circus / London Road. 'H' = New England Street.

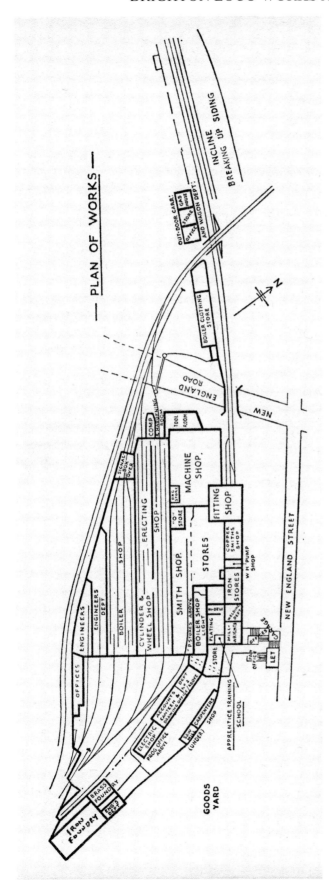

Stores before going back on a lathe.

One of the foreman I worked under in the Erecting shop was Charlie Stuvold where we used to erect the motion onto new engines and fit piston rings to the liners, set the gaps and gently put them onto the valve heads, which, since they were made of cast iron, were very brittle. Next the pistons were assembled onto the crosshead and piston rods, followed by the slide bars, brackets for expansion links and links fitted, and supporting bearings for the weighbar. All the necessary bolt holes had to be reamed out before the actual bolts could be hammered in. Last came the reversing gear itself - Brighton was involved in the construction of a batch of Standard Class 4 tank-engines at this time and the reversers for these were referred to as 'Bacon Slicers'.

After this came the actual valve setting which was normally done on rollers. To achieve this it was first necessary to determine the piston bump marks, and inner and outer dead centres and clearances in mid gear. Feelers were then placed between the leading valve ring on the front of the forward port opening and the necessary openings determined. Next the valve spindle sticking out forward had a horizontal line drawn on it with a box bar. Then a bar was placed over the valve cover bolting face and lines drawn dissecting the horizontal one. If the opening was not correct, the eccentric rod was altered in length. It would be first dismantled before being taken around to the Smiths Fire and Steam Hammer where it was heated and hammered out longer or shorter, while taking into account keeping any offsets correct. Trammels were used to determine length and changes.

Engines for 'Valves and Pistons' had to have the liners and ports de-carbonised. This was done with a hammer and cold chisels and was quite difficult. Sometimes a worn liner needed removing; was done by taking out the 'location' screws after which a long screwed bar was put through the valve chests with a large plate fitted over the cover faces. The forward end of this bar had a large nut, and a ratchet spanner, tube and rope on its end. Sometimes they wouldn't budge and the only way to get the liner out was to chisel between the ends and port bars, a long and laborious process. Cylinder liners were also bored using a portable machine.

Axle-boxes and Horns

Axle-boxes were fitted into the re-furbished horns using an 'axle-box ladder'. This was a short metal

Left: - As works apprentices we were also responsible for conducting tours as necessary. These started and finished at the Canteen steps. The site covered some 9 acres and the main Erecting Shop was 600 feet long. In 1952 650 staff were employed. It celebrated its centenary in 1952 and for which a brochure was produced the cover of which is seen on Page 75.

The entrance to the works for office only staff and off the end of Platform No 10. To the right the wooden doors afforded access to the south yard. The top floor included the Tracing office, CME's office, No 1 Drawing Office, and the Printing Shop.
                                                                          Howard Butler Collection

ladder supported at 90° to the floor. A long wooden pole was put through both this and the un-machined axle hole and then lifted up into the horns. These had to fit, so the axle-box would stay up and when encouraged, slide very slowly down to the horns – some fit bearing in mind the actual weight of the axle-box itself! Horn keeps were used to hold the whole assembly in place.

The main frames had datum pops either side of the centre line of the 'driving' wheel. One put a trammel from one of the pops on either side onto a piece of strip metal which was then hammered into the rough axle opening. This would determine the centreline after centre popping and from which, with a trammel of the correct coupling rod centre lines, the leading and trailing boxes centres could be determined. (Trammels were precision pieces of set lengths and had ground spikes welded on at 90° to a length of tubing. These were collected from the Toolroom Stores as were taps and die nuts.) Axle boxes for repair would first have the diameter of the axle itself measured with callipers, after which they would then go off to the machine shop to be

bored as necessary.

Smoke-boxes

This job involved the removal or replacement of Main Steam pipes, Blowers, Blast-pipes, Superheater Elements, Petticoat Pipes and Chimney bolts. It was a very dirty job and one normally worked through the lunch hour and then went home slightly earlier. Often the nuts were difficult to remove and many had to be cut off with a chisel.

Boiler Mounters

I worked in this gang for about five months when Mr Blount was the foreman in both the Erecting Shop and the Boiler Shop. The work involved tapping out and fitting the studs to the pads on boilers, which had previously been filed flat and scraped to surface plates. We also fitted these to the surface plates. The fitting of Regulators and Rods, Glands and so on sometimes involved working inside the boiler when riveters were also working. The result was that one had

1957, and the last locomotive built at Brighton No 80154. At this stage the engine is on rollers for valve setting. At one time the author had his work bench alongside the wall near to engine buffers.

Completed in march 1957, 80154 was first allocated locally to Brighton and was withdrawn from Nine Elms just ten years later in April 1967.

Centre:and lower - Two views of the completed engine and with (centre) fellow apprentice Geoff (?) leaning out of the cab. Behind the engine is the boiler clothing store.

.

This batch of BR Class '4' tanks were not the only large tank engines built at Brighton in BR days as the works had also constructed 41 of the LMS Fairburn 2-6-4T engines. This was to cover an urgent need for large tank engines for the Southern Region. Leaning out of the cab in the lower view is fellow apprentice, Tony.

Cab view of a BR Standard Class 4 - 80046 in September 1952.

Unless otherwise stated all photographs are from the Author's collection.

80046 depicted at Brighton Shed and ready for revenue earning service. This was also another engine on which I had gone on trial to Lewes. This locomotive had been completed before those shown on the preceding page and hence has the earlier crest on the side of the bunker.

a constant ringing in the ears – no wonder that boiler-makers often became deaf!

Superheater Headers were usually tried up in the Erecting Shop. By this time, boilers and smoke-boxes were normally on the frames. Two long square lengths of timber were partially inserted into two of the empty Superheater Tubes. The header was slung and craned onto these and 'walked' up the already surfaced up face on the Tube-plate, bolted up after applying marking, removed and faced up, and so on. All joints were 'face to face' using a boiled oil and red lead mix.

At this time, we also modified a number of boilers for W/C and B/B locos, moving the safety valve positions to the rear of the boiler drums and substituting two rather than the three valves originally fitted. At the same time these were set for the reduced pressure of 250 compared with the original 280 psi. After a hydraulic test, these were steamed like all other tests on the boilers in South Yard for testing and final setting.

West Country/BB (Original)

Working on Oil Baths first involved the removal of many split pins and nuts. All Motion Pins were secured with circlips, of either inner or outer variety; these items were put in with circlip pliers, which initially took some careful handling since the circlips could fly off all too easily. The West Countries were interesting locomotives, but some had very difficult places to get into, for example, under the Smoke-box and through the Front Plate to get to the Inside Cylinder and 3/8 Rocker Levers.

The Valve Plungers lay between the inside cylinder rear and the oil bath front. There were a lot of small set screws that required removal to obtain access behind the panelling. You wouldn't believe the muck in that location, it was a mixture of smoke-box ash, track dust and oil that got everywhere. A boiler suit could soon stand up on its own! I had some ex War Deprtment Canadian Surveyor's type overalls, which had straps that fastened at the ankles, wrists and neck which helped to

Above: - Brighton Works Open Day 27th August 1952. Behind 34047 is 80044. As well as taking general visitors around the site on that day (- a regular job for the apprentices), I had the privilege of showing my Father and Grand-Father around the works. Grand-Father was himself a former railwayman having been a Chief Goods Clerk on the LBSCR at Tunbridge Wells and Eastbourne.

Below: - Brochure produced for the Works Centenary in 1952.

BRIGHTON
LOCOMOTIVE WORKS

keep out quite a lot of the mess. I also wore toe-protector boots, these had the metal caps on the outside of the leather and resulted in me being called 'Twinkle Toes', but were hardly dainty at a size eleven!Later would come a good wash with caustic soda soap - this was after a good clean in paraffin and didn't do wonders for the hands, especially if there were any cuts.

Other Erecting Shop jobs involved work on the tenders and tanks and which also meant being inside the tanks at times. This was not a very pleasant job in the confined spaces, even less so with the various anti-surge plates and limber holes to get through.

Water valves were fitted to the studs at the bottom plates of tender or tank. They had rubber joints and all studs had washers and were fitted with grommets that were hand made of rope covered in red lead and boiled oil to make them watertight. Again the nuts on drag-boxes

75

32426 at the southern end of 'E' bay on 24th March 1957 and in the process of being dismantled. This engine had been withdrawn in August 1956 after 44 years of service.

V.R. Webster / Kidderminster Railway Museum 018542

normally had to be cut off.

Wheel Gang and Southern End of the West Erecting Shop

The foreman here was little Charlie Henderson, who may be seen on the photo in the Brighton and Hove Gazette of May 1st 1954 with a patch on his boiler suit.

Profile gauges were used to check for tyre wear and thickness when a loco first arrived outside the works, and to determine whether it was turning or new tyres that were required. We used to fit collar nuts to the crank pins and the taper pins that secured them, both of these always being new components. Wheels were stacked both on the rails and staggered between. This was to save space since there were no pits in this area. Eccentrics were bolted to the axles; the holes in them plugged with lengths of 'dowel' and lead poured from above near the face of the eccentric straps.

Arrival at Works

Any engine coming for attention always arrived with its chimney facing south. Tender locos were first separated, which entailed separating the hoses for water, and also the vacuum or Westinghouse air pipe. The drawbar nut, spring and rubber pads were then removed

using a huge ratchet spanner and a few thumps. This took place down in the pit using a 28lb sledge hammer and in winter this could be very cold work and possibly wet too from the now uncoupled and leaking hoses. After 'loosening' a tube and ropes were attached to the spanner and with several of us heaving on them the nut would be undone. The pits in the Erecting Shop could be very cold if the doors at the end of the shops were opened. One was glad of a swift 'warm' at one of the various rivet fires around – little coke braziers from which the boys tossed the rivets to the riveters, who caught them in tongs. The pneumatic rivet guns must have played havoc with their users whose facial expressions told all!

Brass Finishing Gang, Finishing Shop

Harold Ward was the foreman when I worked here, producing sand traps, all cab parts, ejector steam valves, blowers, sanding valves, injector water and steam valves, as well as undertaking repairs to injectors including exhaust injectors with cones. Ejectors for Standard tanks were received complete from makers, Messrs Cravens.

I did the fittings including all the hand-wheels for 80084 which went to the International Railway

The Brighton works Shunter, DS377 receiving attention inside the Works on 24th March 1957. Following the closure of the works, the engine was returned to capital stock as BR No 32635 in January 1959.

V.R. Webster / Kidderminster Railway Museum 018543

Congress Exhibition at Willesden Roundhouse in 1954, and which I also visited later. Harold said; 'Make these a bit special'. We always put a pretty good finish on things anyway, but when I had made all the parts, he inspected them and said, wryly; 'I said it was for an exhibition, not a '.........' museum!' They must have been okay then. We also fitted the oil keeps in the axle-boxes. The sand, which still adhered to the bronze castings, used to wear our files out very quickly.

Several parts for the Standard tanks which we were building came in from the other Southern Works, for instance; tanks cab assembly and frameplates. These would arrive by train of course and the wagons or vans of parts would then be shunted from the Station through the South Yard.

Bunkers were produced in the light Plating Shop. They were all welded and one had to go through this shop shielding your eyes on the way to the Training School.

Frames

These were checked for straightness with long steel straight-edges and, if required, were hammered where needed. Horns were fitted and then set up in screw jacks supported on large baulks of timber stretching across the pits and which were then adjusted for level and squareness. Since all holes were undersize,

temporary stretchers of tubes with welded-on flanges were fitted. The proper stretchers and cylinders were then fitted, the holes opened up and reamed and the fitted bolts driven in. This method was used to overcome the raking stresses set up during service.

The Drillers used drills driven by compressed air as were other most other tools, such as grinders and so on. The drill pillar with a palm was bolted up to the frame, the drill then placed to the hole and the propelling screw taken to the back plate having first set the drill up squarely in both directions to the frame.

Cylinders were fitted after being lined up with the centre line of the driving wheels at the correct angle. Motion brackets, tank and bunker supporting brackets and stays across from the bottom of the horns left-hand to right-hand transverse boiler/smoke-box were fitted. Then came the cab and tanks, bunkers, the motion set up, cab fittings and floor and various pipe runs for injectors, brakes lubrication and others, all the latter in lovely shiny copper.

Painters

I remember the painters doing the tanks and their lining at the lower end of the east bay. Lining was also done by stretching a chalked string line at the correct distance from the edges, then 'pinging' it to use as a guide for the lines. Fitches were used which were very long haired brushes of about 3' or more. It was magic to watch the confidence of the painters. Other painting was also done in-situ.

Lagging on the Standard tank-engines was mainly in the form of glass fibre mattresses, but some parts were asbestos, for example in fire-box flanged plates, and throat and back-plates where a mix of wet asbestos was thrown on these areas. It was the only way to make it stick before shaping it with a wooden spatula. Most other boilers were all asbestos lined.

Loco Classes worked on at this period

During the period I was at Brighton I worked on a number of different classes including, H2, C2X, E1R, E2, E4, E5, M7, Z, T9, S15, N15X, and 32329 prior to the special SLS trip of 23rd June 1956, 'Schools' , Q, Q1, W.C., B.B., and 'Fairburn tanks', before they went off the Southern, and the Electric locos; 10000, and 10001 (we also built 10203). I sometimes assembled, set and tested the fuel injectors for these and also stripped various heating boilers and so on. The smell of diesel was most unpleasant.

Scrapping

Several 'Urie' 'Arthurs' were scrapped during my time. I retained their nameplates for safe-keeping in my locker and hoped to be allowed to buy one, but all of them had been spoken for, so one of my favourites, 'Maid of Astolat' slipped through my hands. This was a very sad job; the tenders went to the former Brighton line six wheeled 'Arthurs' which by then had been transferred to the Western Section.

Trials

In the Erecting Shop, the men worked in gangs and engines were designated to a particular gang. Later when the engine went out on trial two of the gang went with it. I was fortunate in going out on many trials, always to Lewes. The trial driver was Bill Long, mentioned in the Leader books, and his fireman was Les - who didn't mind a spell sitting down whilst you fired. I remember coming down Falmer Bank on a 'Schools' at about 90 mph rolling all over the place. Bill was put 'on the carpet' for this one!

The only unpopular trial was on a C2X if it was cold, wet and windy, due to the exposed cab when running to Lewes tender first – not many volunteers for this one! We carried a kit of tools and had a good check round for anything running hot when at Lewes, but there were never any problems. On a new engine, the smell of warm paint and oil was unique!

Westinghouse Shop

This was the last shop I worked in. It entailed a lot of accurate facing up work on air and steam cylinder ends and their covers valve faces and so on. There was a test rig on which completed pumps were run, making lots of 'pah, pah, pah, pahs'. We also did some water scoops and their operating gear for a small batch of the

Sylvia tracing my axlebox drawing for the Bo-Bo electric design in 1958.

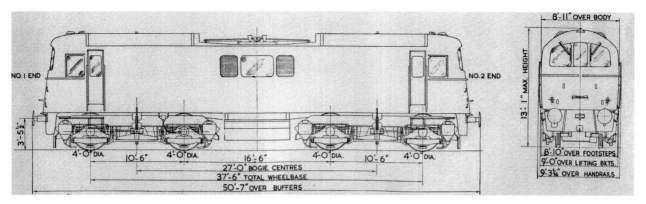

My 1958 drawing of the Bo-Bo Electric Loco type prepared in No. 1 Drawing office at Brighton. These engines were subsequently built at Doncaster.

Standard tanks. At the conclusion of my apprenticeship I was deemed a time-served fitter – but only worked as such for one week!

Fellow Apprentices

The apprentices at this time included Brian Braisher, Max Millard, Geoff (who came from an ex GWR Works), Charlie Painter, Dave Yendall, Dave ..??.. (from Emsworth), Allan Attack, Allan ..??.., Tony Beadle, David? Evans, Tony ..??.. (from Redhill) and Les Warnett, who was about four years our senior.. We had a few outings arranged to engineering works and places of interest whilst in the Training School, which included: Derby Works, where we saw the new Standard 5 4-6-0 being built and the old Lickey Banker 0-10-0 'Big Bertha' that was in the yard awaiting scrapping. Rugby Test Plant: Unfortunately when we got there the 'Crab' 2-6-0 that was on trials had broken some rings, so we didn't see the rollers in operation, but John Click was there and showed us around. This was before he went to Ireland with O.V.S.Bullied on the Turf Burner project.

To the Drawing Office

I started in No.1 Drawing Office on 22nd July 1957. There was another facility – appropriately called No 2 Drawing Office sited in the block above the entrance from New England Street, adjoining the Canteen Block. No 1 Drawing Office was on the top (2nd) floor of the Office Block sited on the west side of the South Yard and abutted the rail lines to Lewes and others. The entrance was from the South Yard. The works manager, Mr Granshaw, had an office on the ground floor along with other offices. The only time I was ever in there was at my interview prior to starting my apprenticeship.

The front part of the entrance block also formed the stone stair well. The stairway started on the ground floor, ascending the north wall towards the east face, the entrance, then turned across this and up the south face to the first floor. Offices lay off to left and right and on the wall facing was the nameplate of 'Remembrance', the original plate from its days as a tank engine. The stairs continued similarly to the second floor, where No 1 Drawing Office was on the left. Ahead was the office of the Chief Mechanical Engineer, Mr Jarvis. To the right were the Tracing Offices, an all - girl team headed by Miss Burleigh. Our own drawings were done in pencil on tracing paper and the girls traced these off in ink onto linen using stencils for all the hand done letters and numbers.

As one went into No 1 Drawing Office there were six drawing boards on each side, those to the left faced south with windows overlooking the South Yard, those on the right faced north and the windows overlooked the station approaches.

My board was the third on the left hand side; the first board was for Mr W.J. (Joe) Hutchinson and the second for Mr E.R.J.Barnes, to whom I was directly responsible. On the other side at the far end was Alistair Lawson, who did all the weight calculations from the drawings produced. Returning back towards the entrance was Derek Marsh, Derek Chapman, Tony ..??.., Frank Knight, ..??.. a junior draughtsman, Jimmy Jones and some others whose names I am unable to recall.

The boards were on cradles to angle them and placed on top of desks. On the right was a space for reference books, drawings and rough books in which one made calculations and sketched out ideas. I usually drew mine in perspective and R.G. Jarvis commented that he could always see at a glance what I had intended. In between the boards was a central passage and several plan lockers containing drawer upon drawer of loco designs! At the southern end was a door through to the printing rooms and the toilets.

The first drawing I remember doing was a rebuilt Merchant Navy Class. I did front and plan views showing it inside the loading gauge and also the throw over on a curve; these were for the benefit of the Civil Engineer. To do these I assembled my drawing from all

SOUTHERN RAILWAY

WORKS MANAGER'S OFFICE,
BRIGHTON.

O. V. BULLEID,
CHIEF MECHANICAL ENGINEER

G. H. GARDENER,
WORKS MANAGER,
BRIGHTON.

TELEGRAMS:
"LOCOMOTIVE. BRIGHTON."

TELEPHONE:
BRIGHTON
6211

REFERENCE.

MY

YOUR

the relevant separate items, an interesting good start.

Other steam drawings included the arrangement of Rocking/Drop Grate for a rebuilt Merchant Navy class, and the arrangement of the Cab Roof Ventilator for the same class, to replace the old sliding ones which could often stick. Normally, arrangement drawings were done last, the items having often already been produced from the actual parts drawings and fitted onto the engines. I remember Tony Beadle who was in No 2 Drawing Office coming over to show me his arrangement drawing of valve gear for a rebuilt Merchant Navy at a time when the engines were already running. I also did arrangement drawings for Automatic Warning Systems and Train Control Systems for various Standard classes, including the 2-6-4 tank and Standard '4' 4-6-0. On one occasion I went over to the Engine Shed and sat in the driving seat of a 2-6-4 tank to determine the best place to site the various items involved, (the Works had since produced its last member of the class, 80154).

I recall commenting on the awful look of the double chimney on the Standard Class '4' 4-6-0 to a chap who was drawing this and working under Jimmy Jones. He told me to put my money where my mouth was – so I did! Hence the chimneys fitted at Eastleigh to the engines of this type we had on the Southern were a much shorter and certainly better looking chimney.

By now most of our work was on the future BoBo Electric Loco to be built at Doncaster. There was a full size mock-up of the cab in the Carpenter's Shop, also a large-scale model of the Crosti-boilered 9F, Boiler Smoke-box, Cab Platforms and Side Chimney; another previous Brighton design.

Drawings for the BoBo that I remember doing included both types of Axle-boxes (Timken and S.K.F.), various drawings of sides, windows (Beclawats), and grill openings, and the flooring (using Kynal tread-plate). Parts of the floor had to be removable for access to all the cabling and piping below, which also had to be suitably supported and, of course shown in reference on the drawing.

Ducting arrangements drawing were made and intended to take air to cool the traction motors down from the side grills. Also included were inspection doors and angle stiffenings all in aluminium and riveted. I remember drawing the openings for these with rounded corners to stop stress cracking, which was normal practice. I was almost finished when Mr Durban, the Chief Draughtsman, told me to make the corners square. I offered my reasons, but was told to do it his way. Having altered all these, Mr Jarvis saw the drawing again and said; 'You had rounded corners originally. Why have you altered them?' I told him and he said 'Draw it as you had it in the first place', so I had to alter them all back to the original version! I told Dick Barnes about this and said 'What a waste of time!' He replied 'Well Brian, it's only on paper. You should have been here in Bulleid's time; he was for ever going to Eastleigh and returning with lots of changes and ideas!'

I felt quite privileged to draw the weights diagram , although I was told, 'Don't make it too pretty' by, yes, you've guessed – Mr Durban!
Most of the Drawing Office team, including Mr Jarvis, were rail enthusiasts and as I was also keen on art were interested to see some of my paintings and drawings. Sometimes I might doodle at lunch time and perhaps a diagram of a rebuilt West Country would acquire a single chimney, or a Duchess type a double, with different deflectors or none at all and so on, even brass-edged hand holes or no handrails. If Mr Jarvis saw these he was quite amused and might say, 'We thought of that one'. I found Mr. Jarvis very fair, friendly and certainly, a gentleman. He once lent me some design books from his office, on American and French Loco designs.

Miss Burleigh, from the Tracing Office, retired whilst I was in the Drawing Office and I was asked if I could paint her a card. She was fond of the Wiston House Lake and Chanctonbury Ring area, so that's what I painted in watercolours for her and it was signed by all in the Drawing Office.

All drawings were laid out in a specific way,

and all the parts were given a No./Drwg.No.in a balloon. The bottom right hand contained the drawing number, date, drawn by (initials), checked by (initials), and down the right hand edge from the top was an amendment column, 6' in total with date and brief reference to what had to be done. Across the drawing at the bottom were parts and numbers required, for example, nuts $^3/_8$' 40, Washers $^3/_8$' 40 and so on. The larger drawings measured to the inner border were some 6'8" long by 3'2" deep, with an outer border of ½'. Scales were usually 1½' or 3' to the foot or even full size for details. The parts around the actual drawing that was done in full line, were drawn in chain dot -.-.- and this was referred to as 'juxta'.

I left the Drawing Office to do a much deferred National Service stint and soon afterwards the Works closed totally as did the Drawing Office. As a result, I never returned to the railway and instead pursued a career as a Marine Engineer Officer in the Merchant Navy.

In these notes is a letter from Mr R.G. Javis in reply to one that I wrote to him shortly after he retired. This letter is much treasured. I have also been glad to see the recent publication of a book on his life and work, a copy of which was given to me. Much appreciated - thanks Simon.

When I started one could not possibly foresee the sudden demise of the steam loco and the terrible scrapping of locos only a few years old. What a waste, and all political!

As long as I can remember, I've always been a railway enthusiast and wanted to be on the design side, seeing the products of the Works emerge, such as West Countries, BB, Leader - yes, I saw this running on trials, Fairburn 2-6-4 tanks and the Standard tanks from 80010.

Also as a lover of all the lovely Brighton designs including Ks, H1, H2, J1, J2, I1X, I3, and B4X I used to view them in the Shed Yard from Howard Place and on the turntable from New England Road. In the shed, we were close up and often in the locos' cabs. I never thought that it would have been cut so short!

Nowadays the Works site is a car park and since returning a few years ago to Sussex, I have walked around the area several times, trying to recall what went where, although little has survived. At the north end was a concreted over road, which followed the exit line 'centre road' of the Erecting Shop East Bay. There was still the handrail and steps down to the position of the toilets under the Tool Room, the bridge over New England Road, where we sat at lunchtimes and a few electrical starter boxes from the tool room site.

From the wall at the east side of the Machine Shop, you can see the piers which supported the Fitting Shop, Coppersmiths, Westinghouse Pump Shop, Millwrights and the Training School. The steps up from New England Street entrance are still visible as is the bridge across the goods line and that at 90° facing south. Before, it used to go through and on to the South Yard. Also the Pay Offices on the bridge remained.

I went back recently to take a photo of these only to witness instead some cranes breaking up the Pay Offices. I had to come away from the site!

I can now only think of happier days and times and of the people that I worked with. I still continue to make locos today although nowadays in 4mm rather than 12 inch scale.

@ Brian Newby Potts 2004

Brighton Works cat. Circa 1938.   *Howard Butler Collection*

FROM THIS -

- TO THIS

IN NICE EASY STAGES...

SO FIRST TAKE YOUR ENGINE...

Then find a suitable place to rebuild it, some skilled hands - oh, and a few ideas of what to do as well……

Following on from the article, 'Early Trials and Tribulations with the Merchant Navy Class 1941 - 1946' in the Preview Issue of 'SW', we were contacted by former Eastleigh Engineering Apprentice Mark Abbott, and who showed us a selection of views of the rebuilding of the first of the 'Merchant Navy' class in 1955/6. How could we refuse? Seen here for the first time are Mark's photographs of the rebuilding process of 35018, most also taken during the lunch-break at Eastleigh Works, hence there is no one around.

Top left: - 35018 'British India Line', the first of the class to be rebuilt, awaiting entry to the works on 16th November 1955. At this stage the engine had run 504,900 miles and been in traffic ten and a half years. A week later the engine was inside the works with the boiler removed…..

Lower left: - In revised form at Southampton Central on 21st February 1956. The small tender emblem was superseded by the 'demi-line rampant' later in 1956. 35018 was one of only a few members of the 'Merchant Navy' class to appear in rebuilt form with the older style BR decal on the tender.

Right: - 28th November 1955 inside the works and already stripped almost bare although two of the frame stretchers were still in place. Mark recorded that three days earlier both the outside cylinders and the buffer beam had been removed. Notice in the photograph that the original middle cylinder has also been removed. Mark's attention to detail has also recorded details of the locomotives alongside on this date and which included 34079, 30837 and the frames of 30773.

7th December 1955 and the main frames are ready for the necessary alterations which are highlighted in white. Some of these will involve cutting whilst in other areas new holes either have or will be drilled. At the same time as the rebuild, 35018 received a General Overhaul whilst a replacement boiler, No 1116, was also fitted. This time the locos visible in the background are 42099, 30852 and 30773.

The new middle cylinder and saddle temporarily supported on a jig representing the bottom of the smokebox. The two items will be bolted together later. This and the next illustration were recorded on 8th December 1955. On this date also work on the frames was continuing with drilling of new bolt holes whilst some metal was also being removed at the rear of the frames ready for the cab.

The same components but this time viewed from what will be the front - still upside down of course at this stage. The holes for the bolts and studs will be marked and drilled when the items are lined up - as seen in the next view. As will be noted later, an overhauled boiler was also fitted during the rebuilding and this was reported as steam tested on 9th December. The studs were also in place on the side of the boiler for what would be the handrails.

One week later on 14th December, and the complete saddle has been placed within the frames although at this stage not bolted. Notice also the lifting chains passing through the steam slot the whole having been hoisted into position by the overhead gantry crane. On the side of the ladder is the name of the Chargeman of the New Work Gang in the Erecting Shop, Les Roberts. By this time all the new frame holes had been made and where new cutting had taken place these areas had been cleaned up. Mark also recorded that the front end had been polished. Over the next two weeks major progress was made on the frames and which included replacing the main frame stretcher between the leading and driving axles. Plates had also been added to support the cab.

The end of 1955, 30th December, and immediately recognisable as the new fabricated smokebox but with an original door. It was this particular shape at the front that helped make the rebuilt engines so unique in their appearance and in the opinion of many contributed towards producing what were arguably the best looking Pacific design anywhere. Earlier on 16th December, the crank axle was balanced and eccentric sheaves fitted. Elsewhere in the shops the position of the whistle was raised on the boiler so as to clear the lagging.

2nd January 1956. Middle and outside cylinders now fitted as well as the outside steam pipe, reversing gear bracket and certain motion components. Some of these may be bolted in place whilst others were jacked into position to 'test-fit'. At this stage the various items would be added and if necessary, removed again, as required. What is not widely known is that at the same time as work was proceeding on 35018, 30852 was temporarily fitted with the chimney and petticoat that would later be fitted to 35018. This was for 'test fit' purposes and according to Mark, visually appeared very squat.

6th January 1956. Close up detail of the motion and with the right hand cylinder in place. Notice a piece of sacking has been used to protect the machined surface of the piston rod where it will pass through the gland. The inside of the frames later received a coat of red undercoat.

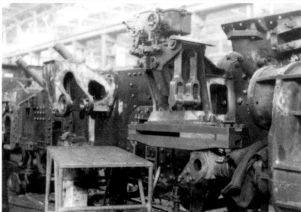

Lagged with asbestos matting but minus cylinders. 9th January 1956. At this stage also the buffer beam has yet to be added. On this occasion also it is No 30841 which is alongside. One week later on 16th January, the first of the brackets to support the running plate were added. Two days later on 11th January the boiler was destined to be taken off again as it was found the shaft operating the reversing gear did not, when fitted into place, correspond with the indentation made in the asbestos matting around the firebox. Also on 11th January the tender was reported as being modified in similar form to that coupled to 34065 and with cut down sides.

On 18th January 1956, boiler No 1116 had been placed in the frames. The presence of the lifting sling around the boiler indicates that it could also be lifted in and out as required. Considerable work has also taken place with the motion, the piston and rod fitted as well as the valve above it - the end of the valve spindle can just be made out. Notice also the mechanical lubricators. The same date saw the reversing shaft referred to above permanently assembled.

One day later on 19th January 1956 and the boiler and smokebox are seemingly attached to each other and with the cylinders added. The ashpan was also in position. In one of the other bays to the right it is possible to identify the cab and frames of 'S15' No 30841. Elsewhere the cab was now finished and resplendent in its gloss paint complete with number. The wheels had also been painted gloss black. The design of the ashpan had water jets available to douse any burning material, these however were only located at the front. Mark's notes record that on a later run (on 10th March) at the head of 9-bogies and a PMV, a fire occurred at the rear of the ashpan and which had to be extinguished from a hose at Brockenhurst station.

Progress now - big time, 25th January 1956. Boiler and cylinders are definitely fitted on a permanent basis as are certain of the motion rods and also the buffers. Notice also the front bracket which will be used to hold the running plate in place. Visible on the outside of the right hand cylinder in this and several other views is the bolted plate that once gave access to the rocker shaft for actuating the valves on the original design. This was now a defunct feature with the rebuilding.

On the same date and now with a chimney and part of the running plate Mark's notes record that on the 23rd January all motion and lubricator gear was in position. The next day, the 25th, the temporary chimney seen here was removed but then put back again and the ejector pipe fitted. The 26th then saw nearly all the axleboxes fitted. Elsewhere in the shops the tender was almost finished.

27th January 1956, the day all three driving wheel sets were finally added. The engine is being lifted to allow the connecting rods to be added. This was achieved by lifting one end at a time and then rotating the respective driving wheels by hand until the rods could be lifted into position.

On 30th January the engine had been moved down the shops and is sitting on the rollers where valve setting is taking place. The rods are lying on the ground and will be fitted shortly to the three driving wheel sets. The whole machine is most definitely looking more like an engine, even the boiler casing and cabside sheeting is now in place. Notice the bogie is not present, this will be refitted later as it is not required for valve setting. This was also the day the tender was painted and lined.

Valve setting was obviously being undertaken on a cold day - witness the stove on the left hand side Superficially the boiler cladding appears to be in undercoat and most of the running plate is present. 30th January 1956.

Final detail of the motion to the left hand cylinder. 30th January 1956.

3rd February 1956. One smoke-deflector added - this had been tried in place on the morning of the previous day but has still to be painted, whilst the hoses on the front buffer beam and all important name-plate are fitted - the plates had been added on 1st February. Due to accessibility problems it was reported that the lower part of the boiler casing was painted and lined at an early stage of the rebuilding and prior to the running plate being added. Later the same day the engine paintwork was given a coat of varnish.

Opposite page - top: Apart from attaching the engine to its tender, it appears complete and resplendent, ready to emerge, 6th February 1956. It was weighed two days later and was running around the works yard, light, on 9th February. Notice there is no handrail to the smoke deflector, this was added shortly afterwards. Between 12.00 and 1.0 pm on 9th February the engine was trialled 'very slowly', light from Eastleigh to Botley. Official photographs were also taken in the works yard. The following day it was turned on the triangle, was again coaled and then left light engine for Nine Elms ready for inspection by the great and the good at Waterloo the next day. On 14th February it returned light to Eastleigh.

Left: - 17th February 1956. Following its various light engine runs, 35018 took its first revenue earning service, the 12.25 pm stopping passenger service from Eastleigh to Southampton Central (9.54 am ex Waterloo), Eastleigh Duty No 253. This duty required the engine to change trains at Southampton Central and take over the 1.29 pm Fareham to Bournemouth West at Southampton. Unfortunately 35018 suffered what was reported as a lubrication problem causing piston valve seizure, and was noted being hauled dead, tender first, back to Eastleigh at 6.45 pm by 'M7' No. 30376. Following a works visit, 35018 was back in action again, light, on 20th February, after which on 21st February it again took over Duty 253 and which involved on M. T. Th., and Sat, the 7.20 am Eastleigh - Waterloo, 11.30 am Waterloo - Bournemouth West, 5.05 pm Bournemouth West - Waterloo, and 10.30 pm Waterloo - Southampton Terminus. Wednesday and Friday involved the single shorter Eastleigh - Bournemouth service and similar return. Unfortunately 35018 failed again on 27th February, this time at Farnborough on the first leg of Duty 353 and due to a buckled RH radius rod. This time is was hauled back to Eastleigh tender first by No 30786. Again the trouble was rectified and which was followed by a successful 9-coach test run to Weymouth. It returned to the same duty as before on 5th March, and this time successfully. It was subsequently returned to its allocated depot at Nine Elms and from 26th March spend 10 days working the 'Bournemouth Belle' which was followed by other turns including the Basingstoke 'stoppers'. The final works visit at this stage was referred to as a 'check-up' at Eastleigh on 14th April and already 5,478 miles since rebuilding. Evidently this was satisfactory as the engine was back in service the next day including working shortly afterwards the 'Bournemouth Belle'.

Above: - 22nd February 1956 and again working the reduced version of Duty 253. The engine was recorded just south of Eastleigh with the entrance to the works, Portsmouth line, and carriage sidings to the right.

Photographs and notes from Mark Abbott. More from his remarkable collection in future issues.

'TERMINUS TIMES'

Continuing the reminiscences of former Eastleigh Fireman, Hugh Abbinnett. Here he recounts a frightening experience at Southampton in 1943.

During my early days as a Fireman on the Southern Railway based at Eastleigh, there were two stations at Southampton. The first was Southampton West, later 'Central', which was used by trains to and from Bournemouth and Weymouth. Access for these trains was via the sharp curve at Northam Junction with the station at the opposite end of Southampton tunnel. I would describe the station as a mediocre collection of buildings; the down side having been rebuilt by the railway in 1934 in art-deco style although the up side complete with its famous clock tower would remain until replaced by British Rail in bland concrete as the 'age of steam' drew to an end. Four main platform faces were provided, the whole area dominated by an enormous electricity generating station which was supplied with coal via the railway from a pair of sidings on the south east side of the site. Facilities for engine crews at Southampton West were nil; small wonder then that the crews of some eastbound local passenger services leaving the station would accelerate rapidly, often reaching 30 mph as they entered the tunnel and in order to reach the second Southampton station at the 'Terminus' where crew amenities were indeed provided.

The other problem with the 'West' was that it always seemed such a windswept place, despite the fact that the 'Terminus' was located equally close to the shoreline, it never seemed to suffer the same gale force winds.

A local crew heading for the 'Terminus' would leave the tunnel maintaining a look out for the right hand signal high on the bracket at Tunnel Junction, for with this in the 'off' position the way was then clear towards Southampton Junction and Chapel Crossing before easing on to the approach to the 'Jack-in-the-box' signal at the Terminus, and which would indicate which platform they were to enter. During the early 1940s local services terminating here would often have an Adams 'Jubilee' at the front, No 642 a particularly regular performer. Having arrived at the 'Terminus' the fireman would have to take care not to let the safety valves lift as this might otherwise disturb the patrons of the nearby South Western Hotel who could look down from their lofty vantage point through the glass roof of the canopy and watch the comings and goings at the station below. (Most of the hotel was requisitioned by the navy for 'the duration' and was officially referred to as HMS Shrapnel.)

'Terminus' also had its own passenger shunter who would uncouple the incoming engine from its train, whilst the station pilot would pull the coaches back before setting these into another platform ready for their return working later.

With the platform now clear the train engine could then run back towards the facilities at 'the loco' where a turntable was also provided. It was to 'Terminus Loco' that I was thrown as a 15 year old in 1943. I had

The exterior facade of the rebuilt down-side at Southampton Central - the tern 'West' had been officially dropped on 7th July 1935 although the former name would stick with railwayman for some years to come. The building seen dated from 1935 but with the main entrance area destroyed by enemy bombs in July 1941.

Howard Butler Collection

already gained some experience at Eastleigh, but as Southampton was a sub-shed of Eastleigh I knew I could also be sent there at any time - as indeed was the case when I was instructed to be at 'Terminus Loco' for 9.00 pm one night.

The actual duty at Southampton involved signing on at Eastleigh at 7.41 pm and catching the 8.16 pm stopping service from Eastleigh. On the way I had the good fortune to meet up with Alfie (Iky) Till, a far more experienced cleaner / fireman (well - by six months!) and it was he who would be my mentor for that first night shift. On the way Iky told me of the duties involved which, because of the blackout, had to be carried out in the darkest of conditions coupled with the ever present possibility of an air raid on the rich target of the nearby docks.

I had with me a copy of the actual duty roster that instructed me 'To raise steam on Engine for 302 Duty ready for the 4.10 am turn at Southampton Town Quay. Also to assist on 308 Duty – up Mail engine and clean as required, 321 Duty - Carriage Shunting as required, and cover 294 Duty – Southampton Town Quay.' In addition I was expected to act as 'Air Raid Precautions (Telephone) for Southampton Terminus Loco.'

It seemed all so very complicated to a young infertile mind and I was glad my travelling companion could explain matters in a way I could understand.

"302 Duty engine will stand all night on her own. The late-turn fireman will have blanked her fire right down with small coal. About 4.00 am just nip over and bring her up to about 90 pounds pressure by pushing the fire all over the box – she will come up to 100 on her own ready for the crew to take her over to Town Yard and take wagons down to the Quay. 321 is just a simple job, give old 202 a quick clean when she comes in from shunting, the fireman on that one will take care of the rest. The Mail engine will be a 'Nelson', so assist the fireman taking water and shovelling the coal down into the tender. That is about it, not much else normally happens. The important bit is that you are also responsible for 'A.R.P.' duties and must be on the alert for the telephone in the Foreman's office, if it is a 'double-red' air-raid warning, then all lights in the area must be switched off and all fires on the ash roads damped down and put out."

The responsibility on a 15 year old's shoulders began to dawn on me, although the walk in the cold air down the ramp at the end of the platform and the 150 yards to the shed was enough to calm the nerves, and by the time we reached the engineman's cabin with its blazing fire I was feeling a lot better.

After stowing our bags on hooks against the white washed wall, Iky showed me round the turn-table hut, coal stage, and engineman's offices, and also the

location of that all important telephone. It still seemed very demanding, especially as he left me shortly afterwards for his own work. By midnight the exertion and mental stress were beginning to take their toll and we were met up again in the cabin around midnight for a reviving snack.

Having indulged ourselves in our respective sandwiches and cake – Ike was happy to have a piece of cherry cake from my own bag and which I felt was small compensation for the help he had given me - we took a bench seat each, stretching out on the hard wood although at the time they seemed as comfortable to us as the best rooms at the nearby South Western Hotel.......

The hours passed without me knowing, and the dawn chorus had also by now started; however I was only partly aware of this, for with a resounding crash the door of the cabin was flung open as one Mr Patrick Brooks, overalls scrubbed, hob-nail boots shining and with thick soles firmly studded with steel protectors, strode in with the intention of indulging in a reviving brew of tea.

'Brooksie' had just arrived as a passenger from Eastleigh on the footplate of No 851 running tender first and, having endured those six miles in what was a cold and breezy environment and being none too impressed with the experience thus far, was understandably seeking a warm reviver. In addition, unbeknown to me he was also the booked fireman for the Town Quay shunting engine, the one I was supposed to prepare and have ready for him with 100 psi on the clock to collect the first rake of wagons from Terminus yard ready for transfer to the Quay - their contents destined for the Isle of Wight ferry. (The Driver for the same duty was due to book on at Southampton shortly afterwards.)

I had never met 'Brooksie' before but he was a big lad, and having just woken up I was, to put it mildly, in a somewhat stupefied condition and no way prepared for the tirade he was about to utter, "….I suppose you call this having my engine ready nipper…?". (The use of this form of identification was not lost on me as he was just eight months older!) "You won't get it ready asleep here on the bench".

I was already attempting some stumbled and feeble reply when Ike walked in behind with a cheery, "It's all sorted Brooksie, your engine has got three-quarters of a glass, one hundred pounds on the clock, and the oil can is in the dish on the boiler front warming for your mate, so don't start moaning, the kid's done well on his first night …".

My senses were still only just emerging into focus although I was aware of 'Brooksie' muttering further as he left, the wind completely taken out of his sails so much so that having entered as a lion he left as a lamb, closing the door quietly behind him. It was also dawning on me just how much I owed to Alfie Till;

indeed we would remain life long friends.

Gradually the remainder of the men began to arrive including the carriage shunting crew, and the driver who would accompany 'Brooksie' on the 'B4' – bug, although the way the latter had behaved anyone would have thought it was for a 'Top-Link' duty. Overhead the sky was also losing it blackness as the clock showed 5.30 am. We had one last drink and I was again more than happy that Iky partake of the last slice of cake from my bag. The final task was to sweep the cabin with what was definitely a size eight broom after which we were away to the station to board the six o'clock stopper to Waterloo, from which we would disembark at Eastleigh and then make our way on foot to the shed to book-off. We agreed to meet again on the 8.16 pm that evening ready for a repeat of the same duty, and although I certainly felt more confident that morning I am not sure I would have been if I could have known what was in store for me just a few hours later.

After what seemed just a few hours I was cycling back to the shed, and leaving my bike in the wooden shed alongside countless others. Then, a walk to the station where Ike was waiting at the down platform. The short journey behind 'M7' No 242 pulling its three caches was 'on the cushions' and with the time spent usefully gaining more instruction from my mentor. But as we arrived at Southampton a wail of sirens greeted us

and we noticed that already the crew of the 'M7' had pulled the blinds across to reduce any glare that might be seen from above. Even so the driver of the tank saw us and also knew where we were headed. Accordingly he called: "Jump up lads, I'll give you a lift to the cabin. There's been a double-red here for some time so when you get to the loco, get those fires and ashes damped down and black out the cabin windows".

Neither of needed much encouragement and after shedding our coats and haversacks we set to with a will. As the underdog of the team, I was instructed by Ike to use the hydrant and douse the red hot piles of clinker and ash near the coal stage. The enormity of the situation still did not dawn on me as like a child playing with water I took great delight in using the hose and watching great clouds of steam emerge to envelope most of the area.

Despite the continuous wailing of the sirens, the dreaded sound of aircraft engines could not yet be heard, and meanwhile trains continued to arrive and depart almost as normal. As with all railwaymen, Ike and I had previously received instruction on ARP work, which included how to deal with incendiary bombs - nasty two foot long cylinders containing magnesium and with fins at each end. These would burst through roofs and buildings spilling their contents which would immediately ignite anything flammable nearby. Within a

Left: - The turntable at 'Southampton Loco' in BR days. The houses in Terminus Terrace referred to in the text were beyond the wall and behind what is the Deanery School.

Right: - Air raid damage at Terminus station on 23rd November 1940. Associated British Ports.

very short time a building would be engulfed by an inferno and accordingly we were instructed to deal with any such bombs as a priority; in retrospect, our own safety seemed to perhaps be of a secondary nature.

Fortunately we also had additional help in the form of the dark skinned turntable operator from the depot known to all as 'Chiefy'. 'Chiefy' – not his real name of course, had once been a Chief Engineer on some ship or other but was now a local resident lodging with a railway fireman in nearby Terminus Terrace. 'Chiefy' would not normally be at work at this hour, but if an air raid warning was in place he was required to report to the depot to assist in any emergency, and he also had one particular advantage - physically he was immensely strong.

The three of us stood side by side surveying the scene. For now at least all was quiet. It was also a very dark night yet still the air-raid sirens were wailing. Privately we all harboured the exact same thought, "Perhaps the sirens were wrong, perhaps they would not find us…". Next moment though the telephone was ringing in the Foreman's Office and automatically I dashed across the yard throwing the door back on its hinges as I rushed to grab the receiver off the cradle, "Hello – Southampton Terminus Depot here…".

The voice on other end sounded grave. "Control here, German Bombers approaching your area, is everything blacked out?" "Yes", I stuttered, "All ground fires extinguished, and black-outs applied to all windows in every building, all locomotives sheeted down and secured".

"Thank you", came a polite reply. "Make no stock or engine movements until the raid has passed. Please inform me the moment the raid is over as to

damage or casualties". I was impressed by the apparent calmness of the Controller and, replacing the receiver and closing the door, I made my way back to my colleagues to impart the instructions.

Now seemed the most uncompromising of situations as the other men from the depot were either with their locos or at their own emergency locations, and yet here we were, two fifteens year-olds and one man against totally responsible for the safety of Southampton Loco Depot and about to face the might of the enemy air-force. Were we scared?, Absolutely, although there was little time to dwell on our fear as already came the terrible whine which indicated the first of the incendiaries and bombs were falling on the docks just a few hundred yards away.

Forty-six berth, which was where imported timber was stored, seemed to be taking the brunt of the action at this time. Some of this timber was kept in sheds thirty feet high intended to keep it dry, but these sheds offered no protection from fire and sparks and the incendiary bombs were already doing their worst in what was in effect a tinder-box environment. Within minutes flames were reaching skywards, illuminating the scene for the unfortunate benefit of even more bombers whilst at ground level the glow could be seen for miles around. Indeed I would hear later that the residents of a number of villages and hamlets could see the flames, all commenting from the supposed safety of their rural area, "Southampton's getting it tonight".

But it was only a matter of time before the bombs and incendiaries started to fall close to where we were as well and both of us spent the time either sheltering under the tender of the nearest engine or using long handled scoops, shovels and stirrup pumps –

anything we could to try and keep the fires at bay. For a while too there was assistance from the residents of nearby Terminus Terrace although on occasions they would desert us to deal with a fire at their own homes. All this was carried out with the very real risk of being engulfed ourselves any moment and without even a tin hat for protection.

More flames leapt into the night sky as the bombs found their mark on the shopping centre of Southampton; the sound of explosions and crackling of flames joined by the sound of still more approaching enemy aircraft. Somehow though Ike and I carried on, fortunately sustaining no injuries, until about an hour and a half later the sounds began to die away, as the aircraft engines faded into the distance.

When we found each other again, we were both black from head to toe from ash and clinker from the explosions, although mercifully without injury. Tea was the next priority and we were joined in the mess room by railwayman from all over, all of whom had done their bit but now reckoned like us, that they were entitled to a quick bit of refreshment before getting back to running a service.

In the distance though came another sound, the telephone again, and I was off my bench as fast as I could remembering for the first time I had forgotten to advise control of the 'all-clear.'

Returning to the cabin again the sound was that of more fire engines arriving at the docks which were still burning fiercely. The urgent need was to move as many wagons away from the fires as possible although first the engines used for this purpose would have to be readied. Accordingly Ike and I went from engine to

engine filling boilers, and although not officially permitted to do so, moving the engines as necessary to top up the water tanks from the column, which fortunately had remained intact along with its water supply.

Again, above the din of the engines another sound could be heard, the telephone doing its best to be heard and so I was down from the footplate and dashing off to the office, the receiver picked up ready for 'control' to speak. The same calm voice on the other first enquired as to the state of engine readiness, congratulating us all on our work, but just as I was starting to relax came the chilling words, "...we have information to make us think there may be an unexploded bomb in the vicinity of the turntable. Will you and Passed Cleaner Till investigate immediately and report back as to the exact location so bomb disposal can attend. It is essential this is done immediately so work can proceed without interruption at both the depot and station."

Once more the enormity of the responsibility placed on young shoulders hit me and I could only fall back on the nearest piece of furniture in the office - a hard backed wooden chair which I sent flying across the lino covered floor. The phone was still in my hand, and 'Control', no doubt hearing the commotion was still speaking, "...are you alright? Are you still there? Has the bomb gone off?". Acknowledging that we would do our utmost to find 'the thing', I replaced the receiver and made my way to the mess room where Ike, still with his smoke blackened face was by now sound asleep.

Rousing him I advised him of the latest predicament. He was alert in a moment with a, "You're joking aren't you?

Bomb and fire damage within the docks. This is 'M' warehouse within the eastern docks and close by Terminus Station.

Associated British Ports

I've had enough for one night, it's 4.30 in the morning and I want to go home". For the first time my mentor seemed just the same as me, a frightened kid who, when times got really bad, sought sanctuary in the one place he felt safe. But that time was still some way off and it was the few months of training that now came to the fore as I repeated again carefully the information I had been given, "…delayed action high explosive…", the type of bomb especially intended to cause maximum injury and damage..

Together we made our way towards the turntables, gingerly searching for any sign of disturbed ground or physical feature. It was not easy, so much of the surrounding area was already covered in soil and ash and in the darkness there was no way of knowing whether this was debris from the night's attack or from a shell buried just beneath our feet. Having found nothing so far we widened the search taking in the staff allotments on the north side of the turntable.

Here were row upon row of broad beans and carrots all neatly lined up, almost as if awaiting inspection and we were both careful where we trod lest we later suffer the wrath of a disgruntled gardener. But - horror of horrors - we soon stopped dead in our tracks, for illuminated in the feeble glare of our handlamps and no more than inches away were the sinister grey fins of what we recognised as a 500lb bomb mostly buried in the soft earth of the allotment.

By now I was becoming an expert at dashing to the control phone, although this time Ike was with me as well. Calling 'control' the phone at the other end was answered almost immediately and I quickly blurted out the news at the same time begging the man at the other end to get hold of the bomb squad "fast".

The adrenalin was also now rapidly draining away and both of us partook of more tea before falling asleep on the benches of the cabin once more. Thinking about it later it was amazing how tiredness overcomes fear. We were awakened an hour later by the sound of sirens and bells which heralded the arrival of the khaki-painted three-ton Austin's reversing as close as they could by road to the depot entrance after which a posse of helmeted soldiers moved onto the allotment, although this time with no regard for onions, rhubarb and turnips.

A very young looking officer with Captain's pips on his shoulders approached the closest and taking a stethoscope from his shoulder bag placed the suction cap carefully against the casing of the bomb. In a matter of seconds he announced in a calm manner, "Live and running, delayed action high explosive". A sergeant was immediately by his side with a tool kit and placing a large wrench in the officer's hand the work began to try and make the device safe…..

Ike and I stood transfixed just yards away by the turntable watching the proceedings. None of the six soldiers had attempted to move us and it was the inquisitiveness of youth that made us remain where we were although had of course the bomb exploded we would have been obliterated in a milli-second. The station and yard were also quiet, the crackle of flames could still be heard from the docks together with the accompanying orange glow but apart from that all was still, almost as if the whole area were holding its breath.

It took about an hour before the Caption was able to announce, "Bomb safe", at which point the soldiers moved in to dig out the casing which was eventually taken away.

I could then finally report to 'control' the emergency was over, and that trains could restart, including our own service back to Eastleigh. Another shift was over; another would come later and with it more experience would be gained; and although no experience was ever wasted fortunately this was one incident destined never to be repeated.

Not Southampton on this occasion, but an example of the type of bomb that fell that night near the loco. This was a delayed action device which fell on Syon Park on 7th October 1940 and was eventually removed on 20th November.

WHAT SIZE BANG WOULD YOU LIKE....?

"Memorandum of Detonator tests carried out between Feltham and Staines, 2nd October, 1929.

A train composed of seven bogie coaches hauled by a 'Lord Nelson' class engine (Engine No. 860 Lord Hawke) was run in three trips, viz; two down and one up between Twickenham and Staines. The highest speed when exploding detonators was between 60 and 70 miles an hour.

The weather was fine with a fairly strong wind blowing obliquely across the track, i.e. from near side to offside when running in the down direction.

The official recorders riding on the engine were Mr A Cobb (Locomotive Department) on the fireman's side, and Mr S Barter (Operating Department) on the Driver's side, Mr C N Anderson, Operating Department (London West Division) also rode in a middle position at the back of the footplate in order to check the results.

The detonators exploded, as laid down for comparative purposes, were as set out below.

Although the above gives the comparative results (except No 5) of different types of detonators, it should be stated that all the explosions could easily be heard from the footplate by the Recorders and this fact was confirmed readily by the Driver (Gray) of the engine. In the circumstances it is not considered that the detonators containing 140 grains of gunpowder possessed any advantages from the point of view of hearing from the footplate over those with 120 grains and the Recorders cannot see that a case has been made out, so far as the Southern Company is concerned for altering the standard detonator containing 120 grains of Gunpowder.

It is to be recorded as a matter of interest that Inspector Shaw riding in the rear Guard's brake (7 vehicles) heard only two explosions (recorded as "weak") out of a total of 42 detonators exploded and these two explosions occurred when speed was only about 30 miles an hour (just after leaving Staines Station.)

	NUMBER & TYPE	RESULT
1.	6 S.R. (present standard of 120 grains gunpowder. and 6 G.W. Cos (Kynoch's) 140 grains).	The Southern Co's detonators gave louder results than the G.W. Co's.
2.	6 S.R. (proposed standard 120 grains and 6 G.W. Co's (Karriers) 140 grain gunpowder.	There was practically nothing to choose between these types.
3.	6 S.R. (proposed standard 120 grains and 6 G.W. Co's (Karriers & Kynoch's) 140 grains.	The G.W. Co's detonators gave louder explosions than the Southern Co's.
4.	6 L.M.S. Co's Duplex and 6 G.W. Co's (Karriers & Kynoch's) 140 grains.	There was practically nothing to choose between these types.
5.	6 S.R. Standard Machine.	These were not exploded against any other type but gave very satisfactory results - all explosions being easily heard from the footplate.

Note: In October 1916 an accident occurred at Kirtlebridge on the Caledonian Railway in consequence of which the 'sounding qualities of detonating signals' were investigated by a Committee of the Railway Clearing House. The results of this investigation have not been traced but it would appear the 1929 Southern tests were a continuation of these enquiries and which would be passed back to and subsequently disseminated through the Railway Clearing House..

COLOUR INTERLUDE

A choice this month for the first page of the colour section, and one where in the end we decided both views just had to go in.

On the right, and supplementing Antony Ford's article on the 'Brighton Belle', is the interior of First Class Car 'VERA'. This illustration was originally reproduced in the January-March 1933 issue of the in-house Pullman Magazine 'The Golden Way', and was noted as being in 'Faraday Natural Colour'. - Antony Ford collection.

Below: Steam at Three Bridges and a Tunbridge Wells service. 'H' Class 0-4-4T No 31530 is sandwiched between two 'Push-Pull' sets, to the left ex SECR and to the right ex LSWR - or according to Mike King's excellent recent book, 'Pull-Push' stock. No date unfortunately, but the first of what will be several views to be seen in future issues from the collection of Paul Hersey.

The Midhurst branch left the ex LBSCR 'Mid Sussex mainline at Hardham Junction about 1 mile south of Pulborough and followed the course of the river Rother through some of the most delightful countryside in the south of England. With the Downs in the distance to the south and the Sussex Weald spread out on either side the line ran through farmland with old cottages, woods with ancient oak trees and the occasional small village or market town. At Midhurst the line met end on with the ex LSWR branch from Petersfield but through passenger trains only operated in later years. There was also a branch to Chichester from which the passenger service was withdrawn in the 1930s.

The first station on the branch was Fittleworth, well placed to serve the local village. After many years of neglect this pretty little station is now sympathetically restored as a private house. The next station Petworth was the principal intermediate station with a large yard, goods shed, passing loop and signal box. Unfortunately local landowner pressure meant that the station had to be built out in the country a good 2 miles south of the thriving market town it was designed to serve, effectively dashing all hopes of sustainable passenger traffic. This station had unusual diagonal planked panelling and is a grade 2 listed building. It survives today as a stylish hotel and restaurant with Pullman cars in the platform. The next station was Selham, like the previous two stations also of timber construction. Selham, to my mind the prettiest of the branch stations, was situated on a low embankment in the centre of the tiny village it served. Remarkably it too survives although surrounding growth makes it now very difficult to see. Midhurst station by contrast was a grand affair with two platforms and a bay. It was built to the LBSCR 'Country House' station design, used also for all the stations on the line to Chichester. (Examples of this design survive in the 3 Bluebell Line stations.) Midhurst however has not been so lucky. Although situated on the outskirts of the market town all trace has disappeared under a housing estate. Passenger traffic, which was always sparse, ceased in 1955 but freight traffic, which could be heavy in the sugar beet season, continued into the 1960s when it too declined and ceased. These pictures were taken in the branch's final days.

All views by Terry Cole

Opposite - top: Midhurst station looking towards the tunnel and Pulborough. The bay platform is in the foreground to the left and the lines to Chichester and Petersfield behind the camera. Trains often crossed at Midhurst in passenger days.

Opposite - lower: Petworth station showing the overbridge carrying the main road to Petworth. September 1963

This page - top: Q1 33018 waits for time at Petworth with the returning twice weekly pick up goods. The disused signal box and site of the loop can be seen on the right. September 1963.

This page - lower: Selham station basks in the midday sun in September 1963. This view is looking east towards Petworth with the tiny yard to the left and a long siding serving a cattle dock to the right. After walking down the long drive the weary traveller would be regaled by the welcoming sight of 'The Three Moles' public house opposite.

Fittleworth station looking towards Petworth. Neither Fittleworth nor Selham had run round loops so goods traffic could only be dealt with on the pick up freight's outward journey. Terry Cole - and whose colour views of the branch are featured here, is in the early stages of preparing an all-colour 'Southern Way Special', details will be announced as soon as possible.